PRETTY

a memoir

by Karen Vorbeck Williams

Cover design by Fresh Designs
Edited by Twyla Beth Lambert

Print ISBN 978-1-945419-42-3
ePub ISBN 978-1-945419-43-0

For Meredith and David

AUTHOR'S NOTE

In writing this story, set during the first twenty years of my life, I have changed the names of some places and people, selectively eliminated some of my family members and friends, and combined some characters as a way to tell the story more simply without a cast of thousands. While I have a good memory and enlisted the help of family members' memories, I used my imagination/memory to create dialogue in many of the scenes. I wrote some of these stories soon after they happened and had the benefit of people who saved letters—mine and my mother's—written contemporaneously and in time given to me for safekeeping. Circumstances that would lead to the identification of some people still living have been changed.

1

Running Away

1955

Where Nobody Knows Your Name — Flyte

WHEN FACED WITH big trouble the women in my family always ran away to California. After a "nervous collapse" in 1921, my paternal grandmother left home for Palm Springs and a long rest in the California sun. In 1935, my maternal grandmother's alcoholic husband drove her to pack a trunk and take a train to Los Angeles. And on the last day of May 1955, at the end of her marriage, my mother packed up her three daughters and flew away from her life in Grand Junction, Colorado to the land of golden streets, sunny skies, and mind-boggling fame and riches.

Our first stop was Reseda, just outside L.A., where Mother's sister Dorothy lived in a tract house with her husband Bill and daughter Linda. Immediately following our excited reunion, we disappeared into Linda's bedroom. We couldn't stop chattering and smiling, staring at one another, sharing that extraordinary love that seems to come out of nowhere just because you are related. The last time we'd seen one another was five years before on a family trip to California.

Linda was eleven—the same age as my youngest sister, Gretchen. My sister Susan was fourteen and I seventeen. Linda would share her room with my sisters, and I would have a bed in the guest/sewing room.

At every opportunity, we left our mothers alone to talk about the divorce and where in California we would settle. The Burgess sisters were close, but there was lots to catch up on. Unlike Mother who loved writing letters, Dorothy did not, and long-distance phone calls were too expensive. The only other method of long distance communication was by telegram, and those were kept short and read like this: GETTING DIVORCED STOP MEET ME AT AIRPORT MONDAY 10 PM STOP BETTE. You paid by the word.

The sisters huddled at the kitchen table over coffee or in the evenings at the picnic table on the back lawn with cigarettes and their iced bourbons and water. Sometimes they would let go with their awe-inspiring identical laughter, and everyone within hearing distance had to laugh too.

Aunt Dorothy looked at Mother with worry, as if she was frail and needed handling with kid gloves. At times, Mother withdrew. I guessed she hated answering Dorothy's questions about *why*. As far as I knew, no one except for movie stars got divorced. I didn't know why my parents no longer loved each other. But I knew Mother had literally run away from home. Her divorce was a secret to be revealed only after we had left town. She answered Dorothy's questions with vague remarks. We outgrew each other. We are very different people. We never should have married in the first place. Then she would change the subject to the future or something upbeat like getting tickets to the ballet or theatre in L.A. My sisters and I had seen Mother's despair—her frustration and angry outbursts, her gloomy moods had frightened us for years. Her evasions and pretended ease weren't new either.

We had come from a house in the country outside Grand Junction, where we lived on a dirt road in a remodeled dairy barn. Below the mountains, fields and pastures spread down to the river and the air was dry and sweet. There, the sun rose in a blue cloudless sky and in late afternoon clouds billowed in time to gather up the colors of a brilliant sunset.

Reseda's asphalt streets burned in the hot sun as thousands of look-alike houses crowded together behind postage stamp lawns. To me, it looked like there were too many people. A smelly sea-sopped fog rolled in every night, falling like a shroud over the house. Mornings were entombed in gray. No clouds, no promising streaks of blue, just gray lingering over the rooftops until noon. There were no landmarks, no mom and pop grocery store, no little bakery shop on the corner, no Main Street. The nearest market was the Piggly Wiggly—the silliest name I'd ever heard for a grocery store. If I'd had a car I would have gotten lost in all the sameness.

I didn't have the right words to protest my sudden appearance in the midst of urban sprawl. Not wanting to add any more to Mother's fragile mental state, I kept my disappointment to myself, hoping we would move to a small town. With no authority to make the promise, before I left home I had told my boyfriend that I'd only stay in California for two weeks. I felt guilty for leaving him and wanted to give him hope.

Reggie and I had a serious problem. My mother knew. While practicing teenage magical thinking, I wrote him every day with the news and to reassure him that I would be home before he knew it.

> Mother and I had a little talk yesterday about you know what, but I changed the subject because she looked like she was about to have a heart attack. Have you told your folks? I hope no one reads this—maybe you had better tear up my letters.

While Mother caught her breath and searched a map for a place to live, we girls watched TV with a blond cabinet and round screen. Every evening we slouched around on Aunt Dorothy's carpeted floor or on the mid-century modern lipstick red sofa. All of the furniture matched: blond spindle legs on the couch, blond end tables with identical yellow lamps, and a blond boomerang-shaped coffee table. We'd never stayed in a house with a TV set before. Grand Junction was isolated in the mountains, and TV reception was impossible for years. When it finally arrived in the early 1950s, the furniture store on Main Street kept a TV running in the front window. Evenings, folks coming into town from the country and those on their way home from work gathered on the sidewalk to watch a man in a turban play the organ. He came on after the test pattern—people watched that too. Besides that, Mother didn't believe in TV. She believed her daughters should spend their time reading, studying, or sewing. She didn't want her girls wasting their time on low-brow entertainment.

At home, we could have taken Linda for a swim in the canal or gone horseback riding in the country. My sister Gretchen and Linda, a blond tomboy, became inseparable. She seemed pleased to share her bedroom and loved Gretchen's company. Usually both went around with bare feet, cutoff jeans, white shirts, and short hair.

Aunt Dorothy had her hair cut and styled at a beauty parlor and seemed much younger, more accomplished, and worldlier than my mother. Dorothy had a job. Mother didn't work. Every day, my aunt put on a suit or smart-looking dress and took a bus into downtown L.A. to work as a keypunch operator at a big insurance company. Uncle Bill was not well and couldn't manage a full-time work schedule.

Before I went to sleep at night, I loaded my fountain pen with blue-green ink, propped myself up on a pillow, and wrote letters to friends and my father about how much I missed them and home. I added news about our trips into the city—visiting the L.A. County Museum of Art, seeing Shirley MacLaine on stage in *Pajama Game,* and attending the ballet *The Firebird* with Margot Fonteyn. When I described these cultural events in my letters, I had no idea who Shirley MacLaine or Margot Fonteyn were. If I hadn't saved the programs, I still wouldn't know how lucky I was. All my letters ended with:

> I wish I could come home.
> Lots of love, Karen

Addressing an envelope to my father, I was reminded that I didn't have an address anymore. Every day I wrote him and ...

> Dear Reggie,
> I've been here ten days. Why don't you write me? I don't think it is very fair because I have written you every day and what am I supposed to think? I am so unhappy and I want to come home, but

you make me wonder if things have changed in some way, that you
don't love me anymore. I just don't know where to turn.

I finished the letter with some news and more pleas for a letter and
turned out the light. The sound of the city came through the open
window as car lights crept across the walls. I couldn't fall asleep.

Mother was silent on the subject. She didn't ask if my period had
started. Instead, an uncomfortable silence as pregnant as I was came
between us. I was afraid to ask questions or to think about *it*. The
best thing I could do, I thought, was to sew a trousseau. As if my
future would consist of nothing but labor over a hot stove and
servitude between Reggie's sheets, I made potholders and a baby-
doll nightgown to match. In an attempt to be cheerful, I cut them
from the same colorful cotton print dotted with bright red cherries. I
imagined myself being happy, a wife with my own little house to
keep. I could see myself dusting and vacuuming, washing dishes
and cooking, but I couldn't hold the baby in my arms.

* * *

While Aunt Dorothy was at work, Mother drove us girls to the beach
at Malibu. We parked and entered through a chain-link fence and
scurried off past crowds of tanned bodies to find a spot very near the
edge of the water. Except for the one day on our 1950 visit when we
took off our shoes and pulled up our skirts to wade in the surf for a
few minutes, I had never been to the beach. Sitting down on a towel,
I was hypnotized by the sight and sound of waves coming one after
the other. I didn't want to move. Susan, Gretchen, and Linda were
already wading in the surf.

"It's as if the waves will never stop," I said to my mother, who
sat next to me in the sand. She laughed and reassured me that,
indeed they would not.

Linda swam out past the surf to quiet waters up to her
shoulders. My sisters followed and turned to wave at me.
Astonished by water seasoned with seaweed, fish, and salt, I swam
out. Linda seemed very brave and unafraid, but I asked if there were
any creatures swimming around our feet. She said there probably

were, but they were harmless. Soon she showed us how to body surf. The afternoon passed and we girls never left the water.

Now and then I glanced back at my mother sitting in her swimsuit under a big sun hat reading a book. When she got hot, she walked to the surf and waded in up to her waist. She splashed cool water on her arms, then dipped in up to her chin. Standing again, she looked out past all the shouting, frolicking children to the horizon. She lingered there and I knew she felt alone and apart.

Back at the house I sat down on the front steps and bathed my burned legs, arms, and shoulders with vinegar. As far as I could see, small pink, green, coral, and blue houses baked in the sun under palm trees as straight and sheltering as telephone poles. I could do nothing to change the heavy air or the feeling of being swallowed up in a maze of sameness, nothing about my parents' divorce or being insignificant and missing from home.

Before I went to bed, I asked Mother to promise that we would move to a small town like Grand Junction.

"I don't want to live in the city either." She kissed me goodnight and closed the door.

I picked up my diary. Picturing the waves and the seaweed stranded on the beach, I wrote what might be the opening of a poem.

> Gentle waves carried seaweed to the shore with a silvery kiss and a quiet nudge—goodbye.
> The only thing I like about California is the beach. I want to go home. Or I did. I'm really glad that I found out, before I made a life with Reggie, what kind of a person he is in a time of need. I worry about Daddy. Is he lonely? Does he miss us? He hasn't written either.

Already Grand Junction seemed like a dream. I could hardly believe that we had been away for only two weeks. I thought back to my room at home, to a night just before we left for California. As I was drifting off to sleep, Mother had come to my bedroom door.

"Are you asleep?" she spoke softly, as if what she had to say could wait until morning.

"No." I rolled on my side to make room for her to sit.

"I've been worried about you—and Reggie. You haven't—uh—gotten too serious have you?"

I knew what that meant, but was not about to confess anything. Mother was worried that I might have to marry Reggie. One of my friends was not showing yet, but her parents had decided to move to Utah before anybody found out. She was probably the reason Mother even asked that question.

"No. We haven't."

"You don't date anyone else. You know I wish you would. Safety in numbers, I always say."

She did always say that. She thought that if you saw several boys you were protected from getting *too serious* with one, but I figured I would probably get too serious with several and was safer with one.

Mother closed the door and sat on the bed. She spoke quietly. "Have you started your period yet?"

Though I held my breath in agony at the mention of my period, I didn't lie. "No."

Mother tipped her forehead into the cup of her hand and closed her eyes to the moonlight. She held herself a moment before she let the words come. "I know how you feel. When I was your age I—I was—you know—raped."

Raped? She'd never said anything so personal—so shocking. Her words left me shaken yet thankful that she had changed the subject. Almost relieved that something bad had happened to her, we could talk about that instead. Quickly drawn more to Mother's sadness than to my own surprise, I sat up and put my head on her shoulder, snuggling into the fragrance of her last cigarette and her rose-scented perfume.

"I wasn't raped," I whispered.

"I know. This happened with a boy you love. You do love Reggie, don't you?"

"Yes, of course," I said, even though I wasn't sure. I knew that most of the time I didn't want to marry him—not yet. Drawn to Mother's long-ago shame, I wanted to understand.

"What happened, Mother? Who raped you?"

How could such a thing happen to her? I wanted to hold her, to cry for both of us, but Mother sat stiffly upright, controlling her emotions. I took her hand.

"My date. He overpowered me in the back seat of his car."

I didn't know what to say to her shocking confession. "Did you tell Nana Pearl?"

"No. No!" she said, shaking her head in disbelief, as if she were thinking, *what an idea. Not my mother, not that upright lady.* "I couldn't tell. I didn't dare tell anyone," she said, her voice trembling. "I had to go to school every day. And he was there—in one of my classes— grinning at me." The words tumbled out. She caught her breath, still not looking at me, but her hand felt moist in my hand. "And then— my period was late—I thought I was pregnant."

"Does Daddy know what happened to you?"

Her body stiffened. "No, nobody knows. I've never told anyone but you. Promise you won't tell him." She waited a moment for my reassurance. "I've got to think what to do if your period doesn't start," she said, hurrying from the room.

* * *

After breakfast, I decided to write a last letter.

> Dear Reggie,
> I am glad that my mother forbids me to write you anymore. You care so little for me that you can't even find time to write. Do as you wish, see anyone you want because it is over between us! In the future, I would advise you to play with less harmful toys than a girl's heart. We are moving tomorrow, and I won't tell you my new address. I don't ever want to see anyone from Grand Junction again except for my father.

We weren't moving "tomorrow." That was a lie. My period hadn't started. I counted nine months on my fingers—January. *I'll probably show before school starts and won't be able to go.*

* * *

Knowing her sister had a generous divorce settlement and alimony, Dorothy suggested that we take a look at Ojai, a little town forty-five miles southeast of Santa Barbara.

"If I could live anywhere on earth, it would be Ojai," she said, explaining that Ojai meant *nest* in the native language. "A little nest where you'll feel safe in the mountains," she cooed. In 1937 Frank Capra shot the film *Lost Horizons* there, a story about the lost city of Shangri-La, a utopia high in the mountains of Tibet.

Chattering about what we wished for in our new town, Mother drove north by a circuitous route. She was afraid of freeways, and Dorothy had routed her inland through the small town of Santa Paula. Mother was the kind of driver who went forty miles per hour no matter the street, road, or speed limit. Worse, she blindly obeyed road signs.

Once when she was driving me to camp in the mountains, she crept down the highway at forty passing a sign for Rifle. At the exit sign, she careened off the highway still going forty.

"Jeez, where are you going?" I shouted.

"It said to exit!"

"But we aren't going to Rifle."

Mother pulled up and turned around.

Hope turned to silence as we drove into hills covered in live oak and eucalyptus, oleander, pine, and palms. We saw strange parasitic growths in some of the trees, and Mother said it was mistletoe. In California the kissing greens grew in the trees. At home it came in little sprigs at Christmas time. The mountains rose around us to six thousand feet, high enough to feel almost like home. We drove on toward the valley planted lushly with orange and lemon trees and began our descent. I caught my breath as the town came into view below in the valley. It looked small and peaceful.

On the main street my sisters and I stood under lacy pepper trees at the edge of the park and feasted our eyes on a cream-colored Spanish-style arcade filled with little shops. Behind its red tile roof the Topa Topa Mountains rose out of rolling foothills to bare-rock cliffs, reminding us of the mountains at Redstone, the high mountain village where we spent our summers in Colorado. To the left stood the Ojai Playhouse (a movie theatre) and the post office at the base of a tall Spanish bell tower. Across the street, the elegant-looking Oaks Hotel hid its garden and swimming pool behind a stucco wall. Beyond that, a friendly little grocery store sat on the sidewalk just like the City Market at home. Except for the Big Dipper Frosty Shop, that's about all there was to downtown Ojai—the population was around 3,000, much smaller than Grand Junction.

Mother, an artist, thought Ojai was perfect. It had an art center, Theosophist guru Jiddu Krishnamurti in residence somewhere in the valley, and the "Mama of Dada," the great potter Beatrice Wood in her studio up in the hills above the town. I was more impressed that film stars Bud Abbott, Loretta Young, and Rory Calhoun lived there.

A real estate agent took us to see a house sheltered under a spreading live-oak tree; set back from all the others in the tract it was distinguished by an exceptional garden. The dichondra lawn in the shady front yard looked like it had been lifted lush and green from the floor of a tropical forest. While the realtor explained that it would never need mowing, I went to my hands and knees to examine the tiny cone-shaped leaves—lush green and fragrant. I had never seen anything like it and in the years to come would lie there under the arms of the tree that stretched over our house on Shady Lane. The back garden nestled inside a wall topped by lattice dripping with passionflowers and laid with flagstone under a vine-covered pergola. Beyond the garden gate was an open lot with a perennial stand of globe artichokes and a vegetable garden. Mother was not interested in seeing any other house and made an offer.

*   *   *

One morning, while my sisters and cousin had gone down the street to a neighbors to see their new puppies and Aunt Dorothy and Uncle Bill were at work, Mother washed the breakfast dishes and I wrote a letter to Reggie. I had finally received a letter from him. The postman took my last scolding missile—when I broke up with him—as he dropped Reggie's through the door slot.

> Dear Karen,
> Sorry I didn't write sooner. It's been busy around here. Dad needed me to work and, you know me, lots of parties. Don't be jealous—just me and Dan and the gang. I haven't forgotten that the prettiest girl in the world is in California. Sometimes I drive

out to your Dad's house and watch the sunset. Sunsets are way
more exciting with you. Get what I mean?

The letter went on to describe his choice of a college—*if my period
starts and he gets to go.* He reassured his love and willingness to
marry if necessary and asked me not to be mad at him. It was short,
just one and a half pages, but I was relieved and had to explain.

I am not mad at you, but my mother is. I tried to tell her that
you hate to write letters, but she is mad.

My letter went on to say that we had found the town where we
wanted to live and begged him not to be mad at me because of my
last letter.

Not long after I wrote that letter, when Mother and I were alone,
she quietly approached me in the kitchen. She held two small pills in
her open palm. "Take these," she said softly. "It will make your
period start." She said nothing about a baby—that it would die. I
wouldn't want to think about that and she knew it. Without a word
or a question, I took the pills from her hand, filled a glass of water
from the faucet, and swallowed.

"The doctor said that in about 48 hours you might have some
cramping. If you do, you may want to lie down."

* * *

The house seemed empty. Aunt Dorothy had gone off to operate her
keypunch machine and Uncle Bill to paint houses. Susan, Gretchen,
and Linda played outside with our new puppy. Mother settled on
the sofa with a book, and I went into the bedroom to lie down.
Severe cramps had driven me there.

With my face to the wall, spiraling through darkness and pain, I
lay there a long time muffling my cries in a pillow, thinking of
Reggie. What would he say if he knew what was happening? I hated
myself and hoped the pain would help me forget how good it felt to
have sex. I never wanted it again and understood that it was a
penance for being bad, and for taking the pill that would set me free.

Through the pain I had no concept of time, but it seemed like dusk outside. Maybe evening approached, or a storm was on the way, or I was dying. Then I heard familiar voices and the sound of canned television laughter coming hollow down a long nightmare corridor. I pulled harder on the pillow, smothering cries too shameful for anyone to hear. Not once had Mother come in to check on me nor to comfort me. I had not expected her to, no more than I expected that we would speak of that day ever again. Exactly what happened in Reseda behind that closed bedroom door would be our secret from each other.

Late, when shadows spun across the walls and night echoes came through the open window, I got up to go to the bathroom. Quietly, I slipped across the dark hall. I closed the door and sat down. Something left my body, but I was afraid to look. After I stumbled back into bed, I made a pact with myself to forget everything—to never again think about the pills, or loving Reggie, or the blood in the water.

I thought about my mother and what had happened to us. She seemed different away from Grand Junction. Even though we were unsettled she was calmer and not so sad or angry all the time. Both Mother and I had broken the rules. It was immoral to have sex before marriage, and my mother, who had left her marriage, was ashamed to live in the town where she was born. I knew people would talk—say she was a bad woman.

I didn't think she was bad. But I knew I was.

2

Bad Little Girl

Grand Junction
1940s

"Karen thinks she will change her name to Joan Ann because she is good when she is Joan Ann. When she is bad she is Delma." —Bette Vorbeck, from a letter to her mother

WHEN I WAS two and a half, my imaginary playmate came to live with us in our 1920s bungalow in downtown Grand Junction. My parents were aware of Zackly because I blamed him for all the things I did wrong. When a vase fell off the shelf or milk was spilled, Zackly did it.

A few months before my third birthday I was told that very soon I'd have a little brother or sister. That's when a second imaginary playmate showed up. Little Sister was a marvelous haloed baby who came down from the sky bringing small wisps of cloud along. Little Sister was always good. When she called me on my red tin telephone we talked about that funny Zackly, but I never let Little Sister talk to him. No one else could. I didn't want to hurt her feelings so I never told her that I loved Zackly best.

Zackly didn't budge or raise an eyebrow when my sister Susan was born, but Little Sister floated back to the clouds and I never saw her again. Both my sister and I grew up knowing that my father wanted sons to carry on in the family name and sporting goods business. He was the last Vorbeck in that line. I was supposed to be Charles, and Susan was supposed to be Stephen.

How, you ask, could I possibly remember all this? I don't. That is not to say I have no memory of Zackly or Little Sister. I remember him especially, but not in the detail described in Mother's letters to her mother. Nana Pearl saved every letter. Before she died, she sent them to me. Because Mother's days were spent at home with her children—and she loved writing letters—Mother had a lot to say.

The moment Susan's tiny baby fingers curled in my hand I fell in love with her. She had brown eyes as round and quiet as a kitten's and smelled so sweet I had to bury my face in her neck. Sometimes I wanted to bite her delicious little ears and bend her tiny fingers until she screamed. When Susan cried her face changed into what looked like a furious raspberry. I didn't like her one bit when she cried and flailed her arms and legs like she was trying to swim away.

I told Mother that Susan was more fun than a doll. I didn't mention that I hated the fact that she didn't have any time left over for me. But I did whatever I could think of to get noticed.

I loved Zackly because he came to me when I was lonely. He could change in an instant from a giant to a tiny fairy leaping around the room. Sometimes he landed on my shoulder. After Mother put the cookies away, he cupped his hand around his twisted little mouth and whispered, "Go on, take some more. I dare you." And I would.

"If you can't get Zackly to behave," Mother said, "I'm going to have to spank Karen."

I got a lot of spankings and, in return, I spanked my baby doll every day.

"This," I said to my baby, "hurts me more than it hurts you."

Having two little ones was a challenge for Mother. Sometimes she sent me to stay in the country with my father's parents, whom I called Gommie and PopPop. My maternal grandmother, Nana Pearl, lived in L.A.

At the pretty vine-covered house down by the canal I knew I was adored. One morning after breakfast, when I was busy playing with my baby doll, Gommie came upon the scene. She looked me over sharply.

"Time for a bath, young lady."

"I took a bath already!"

"When?"

"Just before," I said, distracted by my baby's left eye. It wouldn't stay open no matter how hard I poked it.

"Just before what?"

"Don't remember."

"Nonsense. Your hair hasn't been washed in a week. Look at the dirt under your fingernails. I bet we could plant seeds in your ears and get a good crop of flowers." She grabbed me under the arms, picked me up off the floor, and carried me toward the bathroom.

I made myself stiff as a board. "No! I don't wanna."

She sat down on the toilet seat and unbuttoned my dress. "Sit still, Karen."

"No! I can't get undressed." I cried and kicked as Gommie tried to pull off my shoes.

With one hand she turned my head for a look into my eyes. "Why not?"

"'Cause Zackly's in here and he's a boy!"

"Oh, that Zackly," she sighed, trying not to lose patience. "What nonsense. Hold still while I unbutton your dress."

"Zackly's here! Make him go!"

"All right, all right!" She stood and opened the bathroom door. "Where is he?"

"There!" I said, pointing at the windowsill. "There!" I cried, indicating the top of the medicine chest.

Gommie dashed around the room waving both arms, her hands gesturing wildly. "Go away! Go away, Zackly!"

I watched him fly out the door. Gommie shut it tight, and I went peacefully to my bath.

*   *   *

Susan hardly ever said a word because I did all the talking for her.

"Susan doesn't like oatmeal—she wants pancakes." I'm afraid that meant that I wanted pancakes.

Mother thought that if I went away for a while my little sister would have to talk. At one point, Gommie took me away on a train trip to Denver. It worked. Once I was gone Susan found her tongue and kept it.

*   *   *

I heard all the popular songs on the big console radio in our front room. When I was old enough I sang along. When I sang I could feel God smiling at me and clapping His hands. I flew to the sky with the high notes, especially when Mother came to listen and smile her approval. My voice carried a childish vibrato as I imitated the girl singers on the radio.

Closing my eyes I sang, "You made me love you," my face up-turned, my arms held like a bird the moment it decides to fly. Mother watched and wrote, "She sings just as if she knows all about falling in love."

When neighborhood children came to play, sometimes I herded them onto the back steps, made them sit down and be quiet, and turned the lawn into my stage. Even though I couldn't always remember every word, I sang popular songs, or the Doxology, which we sang in church. "Praise God from whom all blessings flow..."

When I ran out of repertoire I made up songs of my own. If the song and dance was silly, the kids laughed and clapped their hands. Sometimes when Mrs. Burke was out working in her garden she peeked over the fence to watch. She told Mother she thought I was gifted and pretty.

Once, after Mother sent all the children home, she brought me inside for quiet time and a story. "What did you sing for the children?" she asked opening my new book.

"Dolly in heaven."

"It was beautiful. Sing it for me now?"

"No."

"Why not?"

"I forgot it."

"You know, I can't carry a tune. I'm tone deaf. But you can sing."

"Why don't you take me down to the radio station so I can sing with the Andrews Sisters?"

When Susan was old enough we played with our storybook and paper dolls almost every day. Mother let us take all the books off the shelves and use them like building blocks to make cities and rooms. One of her high-heeled shoes with a rhinestone buckle made a perfect carriage for our Cinderella doll. Our mother helped us stitch simple doll clothes with a needle and thread. Susan and I made May baskets by weaving pink and green construction paper strips together and filling them with lilacs and spiraea. We hung them on our neighbors' doorknobs. Then we rang the doorbell and ran away to hide with the butterflies in our stomachs.

* * *

Our father worked long hours at the store, but we saw him almost every day—usually behind the evening newspaper. When he listened to the radio, sometimes he would take us on his lap. He smelled like his pipe and the whisky he drank as soon as he got home. Every now and then he tickled me when I was in his lap. I didn't like it because he wouldn't stop even after I begged him. He kept it up until I panicked and couldn't breathe and started screaming. Usually Mother had to tell him to stop. As soon as she turned her back, he looked at me with disgust and whispered, "You are nothing but a big baby," and he would push me away.

I'd go to my room, lie down on my bed, and wish that he liked me. Somehow I thought he loved me. I figured that fathers and mothers had to love their children. And he liked to tell me how I was the most beautiful baby ever born at St. Mary's Hospital. When I dressed up he would say he was proud to be the father of such a pretty girl. Still, I disappointed him all the time. He called me dummy, sissy, and big baby. Mother never called me names; she just yelled at me and spanked me.

I'd heard other children call their mothers mommy or mom. "Mommy" sounded sweet to me. "I'm sorry, Mommy," I said after Mother scolded me. I wanted to make up with her—for her to take me on her lap like I was still her baby.

"Call me mother."

"Why can't I call you mommy?" I patted her hand. Mommy had just the right amount of warmth and expressed how much I loved her.

"Because it's too cute and I don't like it." She looked offended and pulled her hand away. "I'm not cute."

I decided to try for second best. "Can I call you mom?"

"No. That's what sailors call their mothers." She stood and walked away, putting an end to the conversation.

Now I know that to her, "Mommy" meant powdered, perfumed mother in lace and bows—like Mrs. Miniver at the movies. "Mommy" swept the kitchen floor every night and never left dirty dishes in the sink. "Mommy" called her children darling and dearest and sang lullabies to her babies—Mother couldn't carry a tune. Mother, the student artist who drew with charcoal, pencil, and colored inks, who toyed with the idea of becoming a writer and spent every hour she could either writing long letters to her mother or with her nose in a book, was not "Mommy."

* * *

One gloomy Sunday afternoon after church, the family gathered around the dining table for the late afternoon meal. A white winter sky outside the window backlit my father, turning him into a dark effigy. He sat at the head of the table with my mother to his left as they carried on a conversation. I didn't understand what they were talking about, but their demeanor was something I understood. He spoke to her like he spoke to me. She had been bad—I knew that much. Finally he stopped talking. An unbearable silence followed.

Mother's head was bent over her plate as if she was ashamed. Without a sound she put down her fork and folded her hands in her lap. I searched her downturned face and looked across the table where Susan, wide-eyed, was watching.

My father was cold and motionless as a statue.

Tearing chunks of sweet fat off the pot roast with my fingers, I ate as fast as I could, trying to swallow the bitter sadness. Soon nauseous from my greasy feast, I asked to be excused and put myself to bed. I never asked Mother what was wrong, and she never offered an explanation. To this day I can go to the dining room table in my head and feel again what I felt then. As it turned out, our parents never fought. Theirs became a silent marriage.

* * *

In every season but summer, little girls wore cotton undershirts under their dresses. Their shoes were laced or buckled. Unless they were poor, they had dress shoes in black patent leather and oxfords to wear to school. Their socks were white cotton and so were their panties. In summer they went barefoot almost all the time and wore sundresses and sun suits and white sandals their mothers had to paint with shoe polish. Every spring a new coat and hat were purchased downtown in one of the stores on Main Street and in the fall a new winter coat and hat and snowsuit. Mothers sewed new clothes for school and an Easter dress to go with a brand new Easter bonnet. Little girls had mittens and white gloves. Every morning they took a spoonful of cod liver oil, and when they had a cold their mothers made them wear a burning mustard plaster on their chest while they slept. To keep the germs out and prevent colds, a stinging finger full of Vicks was rubbed into both nostrils. Dare a child be constipated for more than a day, she was laid down screaming in the bathtub with a plastic tube thrust up her bottom. Under threat of punishment, she had to hold all that water inside until she was told to sit on the toilet.

Measures like these were taken for our health. Parents did not set out to torture, and they knew nothing about child psychology — nobody did. Children died of infectious diseases and we were at war. Via the radio we heard Hitler's terrifying voice. The Nazis were rounding up the Jews. Suicidal kamikaze pilots dive-bombed American ships. It was a time of insanity and fear.

During the war my neighborhood pals came to play bringing painted zinc airplanes, Jeeps, and tanks. Together we built roads and hills in the dirt and drove our Army vehicles into battle against Hitler. Planes buzzed overhead and bombs fell, knocking the tanks off the road and overturning Jeeps on their way. Our pilots had dogfights with German Messerschmitts and dive-bombed the enemy tanks outside Mother's kitchen door. Lots of German soldiers lay dead in the dirt along our driveway.

It was a long war with its Victory gardens, food and gasoline rationing, the switch from the manufacture of typewriters, cars, and bicycles in favor of munitions, the clothes drives, the imposed 35 mph national speed limit, and the shortages, none of which bothered me — only the disappearance of bubble gum. When the mom and pop grocery finally got some, I lined up with all the other neighborhood kids waiting my turn to buy one piece for a penny. Even if we had a nickel in our pocket they wouldn't let any child have more than one piece. I got my piece, chewed it for days, and put it on the bedpost at night for safekeeping.

In spring, my father and grandfather let me help plant a large Victory garden at our grandparents' house in the country. I understood that if we raised food for our family and our neighbors, there would be plenty of food for the soldiers. I could be part of the war effort.

After the spring rains, we watched pretty shoots of green pop into the sun and flourish as seedlings all over the field. During hot weather, my father and grandfather didn't water the seedlings and all the little plants dried up in the sun. They let that field go to weeds. They had no skill with growing things.

*   *   *

From the kitchen window Mother looked out on the vacant lot filled with summer weeds tilting in the breeze. Eddie and I were playing in the abandoned shed we used as a playhouse. He was a third grader who lived in the house across the lot, and I must have been about five. Mother was learning to draw and had read a book on the development of creativity, and she wrote to her mother about it. The author said that artists of every sort credited their parents for engaging them in conversation when they were young. These gifted people had parents who asked questions about their child's activities and thoughts. As children they grew up knowing how to express themselves. She wanted to know what her daughter was learning, experiencing as she moved around the little shed talking to Eddie.

At lunch, over peanut butter sandwiches and milk, Mother said, "I could see you and Eddie had a nice conversation. What did you talk about?"

"Fucking?" I said, wondering what it meant.

Mother's face turned white, then deep red. "Don't you ever — ever dare say that word again!" She grabbed me by the arm and dragged me across the kitchen. "You need your mouth washed out with soap." Furiously she pressed me against the hard enamel sink. Somehow, even though I struggled and screamed, she managed to stuff a bar of Ivory soap into my mouth and rub it back and forth over my tongue. The taste and the pressure made me gag as I tried to wiggle free, but my mother was too strong.

Violently wiping my mouth with a kitchen towel, she pulled me screaming across the kitchen to the front hall. At the door to the small bathroom under the stairs — with a few swift blows to my bottom — she pushed me into the dark room and slammed the door shut.

"You can't come out until you're sorry!"

Lying in a heap in the dark sobbing, I couldn't catch my breath. My whole body shook as I tried to calm myself, to sit quietly — still confused — staring at a crack of light under the door. I tried to puzzle out this sudden turn of events. Why did one word make Mother look so wild and afraid? *What am I supposed to be sorry about?* It took a long time before I wanted to leave the refuge of that small dark room where my shame was hidden from sight.

* * *

I wore dresses to school, sometimes with a pinafore. Mother braided my hair, plain or French, tied with ribbons. Everyone said I was pretty. I learned to read my first words for Miss Wilson, a slim, thirtyish woman I adored. It felt like Miss Wilson loved me. From our textbooks about Dick and Jane, I learned that Jane was the perfect little girl. Their family had a cat and a dog and a baby sister, and her mother kept the house tidy and never spanked Jane. Her father was patient and kind. He flew a kite with Dick and never spanked his children. That didn't puzzle me. I understood. They were good children—that's why Dick and Jane's parents were so nice.

At first Mother insisted on walking me to school. Hand in hand we walked down Teller Avenue, turned on Fifth Street, and walked one block on Hill Avenue's cracked sidewalk passing parched lawns and houses baking in the morning sun.

Soon I wanted to walk by myself or with other children, skipping down sidewalks hot enough by noon to fry an egg. There were all kinds of things to look out for on the way to school. Once, three big boys on bikes chased me down the sidewalk. I could feel the danger the moment I saw them coming, volatile, sneering, gathering speed. I escaped through the screen door into the mom and pop grocery store just in time. After that, when I walked alone, I spotted hiding places along the way and kept one eye out for those boys. I kept the other eye on the sky watching for storm clouds. I hadn't forgotten the story Mother told me about when she was a kid walking to school. Just steps ahead of her a bolt of lightning came out of the sky and cracked the sidewalk in two. Things like that happened in Grand Junction.

Walking by myself past lawns dry as tinder, across from the school, I saw a shady green lawn under the trees in Hawthorne Park. It looked cool there. I crossed the street and wandered into the shadows where leaves above trembled at the hint of a breeze. Making up a game, I ran as fast as I could around the trees trying to touch every one. The tall trunks, scattered at random, and the welcome coolness reminded me of our summers in the mountains. I forgot, for a while, that I was on my way to school.

I looked through the trees. Across the street, the sidewalks and playground were empty. *Did the school bell ring?* I was in trouble. All the children were in school sitting at their desks with their books open. Suddenly the elevator in my stomach hit bottom. I had never been late to school, didn't know what happened if you were late, and didn't want to find out. I had seen the wooden paddle hanging over the principal's desk and knew it was not for decoration. Sometimes, when I walked by, I heard screams coming from that office.

Finally, I decided there was no place to go but home. I walked for a while under the trees trying to think what lie to tell my mother. On my way home, with Zackly's help, I perfected and practiced exactly what to say.

* * *

"Mother," I said, walking into the kitchen, fully confident of my story. "There's no school today."

"For heaven's sake, why not?" She looked surprised.

"The school burned down."

"The school burned down?" Obviously shocked, she took off her apron, checked her hair in the mirror, and freshened her lipstick. She took my hand and led me toward the door. "Well, that must be quite a sight. Let's go see!"

She walked with me out the door, down the block, across Fifth Street, down Hill, talking about what a sad thing for all the little children that the school had burned down. As she hurried me down the sidewalk she reminded me of all the poor children in the world who wished they were lucky enough to have a chance to go to a nice little school like Hawthorne.

Things weren't turning out the way I'd expected. Mother held my hand tight, and as each step brought us closer to the schoolhouse, I prayed that somehow by magic we would soon smell smoke and find a big pile of ashes. As soon as the little brown schoolhouse came into view I began to cry, "I didn't wanna be late. Please let me go home. I hate school!" Which was a lie. I loved school.

"Shame on you," she scolded, yanking my arm. "You'll be very, very late now." Mother walked faster, holding my hand so tight I winced with pain.

When the door swung open, all the children turned around. Mother led me crying to the front of the room. Everyone was silent. Not a sound was heard except for my sobs. Ears strained to hear what Mother was saying to Miss Wilson. Everyone heard my big lie.

Miss Wilson looked shocked then deeply disappointed. I was not prepared for how bad it felt to disappoint her. My beloved teacher walked to the closet, removed the tall stool, and placed it in the front right-hand corner of the room. She gave me a cross look and pointed.

Mother looked satisfied with the teacher's solution. "It will teach her an important lesson." She bent to look me in the eye. "Take your seat."

I knew what to do. In kindergarten, I saw Jerry Henderson banished to the stool for fighting, but I'd never seen a girl punished that way. I climbed up and for the rest of the day sat there with my face to the wall feeling all the children's eyes on my back, knowing my father would spank me hard when he came home after work.

That night I begged my father not to spank me, apologized for my lie, and said I would never ever tell another lie. I could not keep back the tears as I pulled down my panties and placed myself bottoms up over my father's knees. He picked up the hairbrush Mother had handy for the occasion, turned it over to the spanking side, and hit me with it while I screamed and cried and begged him to stop. Susan watched with terror from the hall, and when it was over and I was sent to our room, she comforted me.

Afterwards, as I lay in my bed, a deep sadness moved over me as weariness crept into my arms and legs. My eyes grew heavy, and I knew what I had to do. Send Zackly away. He made me tell that lie. Besides, I was too big to have an imaginary playmate. My father said so. Zackly had been my close friend, but he was the one who tempted me to do bad things. I couldn't count all the spankings I got just because I listened to him.

I waited under the long straight shaft of moonlight shooting through the gap between the shade and the window frame. "Zackly?"

The light cutting through dark shadows seemed alive with a powdering of dust as Zackly fell on my pillow. "I can't play with you anymore."

"Piffle! Piffle! Piffle!" His little P-puffs of air tickled my ear. He rolled down my shoulder and sat on my chest. "O' course you can."

"No, Zackly, you get me into trouble."

"Sakes alive, we're just havin' fun—learnin' clever tricks."

"Go away, Zackly."

"Don't say that!" He looked sad.

"Never come back again."

"Don't." He was growing smaller. "Don't—not now."

"Go away *now*—and never come back."

Slowly he vanished, like a raindrop drying up in the hot sun.

In the days and weeks that followed I missed Zackly. I lay in bed at night crying, aching for him, telling myself that no matter how lonely I was or how much I loved him, I must never call him back.

3

Alone in the Country

1949

AS SOON AS fifth grade let out, my family moved from town to the country. My father bought three acres of land among neighbors an acre or two away. Almost everyone had enough land to keep a horse, a milk cow, and a vegetable garden. Mother wanted the remodeled dairy barn on a west-facing hill with a magnificent view of the mountains. The house itself was run-down, too small, and in need of modernizing.

Mother needed something new, a road never taken, a house to decorate. Maybe in the country where the breeze blew fresh air into the windows, where the eye never stopped until it reached the sculpted curves of the mountain range, where green pastures ran into fragrant orchards, maybe there she would feel free.

Inside the house, old walls would come down and new walls go up. An ultra-modern addition—an out-sized room with a fireplace and large picture windows, a combination living room, dining room, and kitchen—was a great room before its time.

She chose gum-wood paneling for the living room walls and blond wood for the table and chairs she designed and had built for the dining area. The unusual red and chartreuse striped, textured fabric for the drapes contrasted with the soft caramel and gray earth tones of the woods, the beige shag carpet, and the sandy-colored fireplace bricks. She designed a bench less than a foot off the floor, about the same width but shorter than a twin bed, and covered it with an upholstered four-inch foam rubber mattress. Calling it the "thinking bench," she draped it with a colorful throw for warmth and lots of red and chartreuse pillows. Under a reproduction Alexander Calder mobile and a tall crook-necked floor lamp, the thinking bench was within reach of the new wall filled with floor to ceiling bookshelves. My grandmother said the new room was from the "Good-bye, Mr. Chippendale" school of decoration.

Mother was thirty-four and studying drawing with the artist Verona Burkhard, who had made her living painting post office murals for the WPA during the Great Depression. The daughter of artists, she had exhibited at art museums in Philadelphia, Cincinnati, Los Angeles, and Denver. Her maternal grandfather, Giovanni Turini, had sculpted Garibaldi's statue in New York's Washington Square. Her father, Henri, was a noted painter, and her mother, Vee, a former fashion artist in New York City. Mother had the good luck to find Verona living on a hill off First Street, a quarter-mile walk from home.

Verona was born in Paris but spoke with an exotic New York accent. I sensed her uniqueness and loved going to her studio to paint, sculpt, and make pottery during her Saturday morning children's classes.

Mother had always wanted to move to the country. The bungalow on Teller Avenue had no potential. In town she did her wash in the wringer washing machine in the little room between the kitchen and the back porch, which faced a vine-covered arbor and a backyard half shaded with trees. She hung the wash on a clothesline in a large patch of sun at the back near the alley. The icebox was in that same small room. The ice man came whistling through the porch door lugging a large block of ice.

While Daddy was at work, she kept busy sanding and painting. She cleaned the old wallpaper and made it look good as new, and she sewed new drapes for the front room and café curtains for the kitchen. That house was one of several my father bought, fixed up with Mother's help, and sold at a profit.

While she put her hands to the task of redecorating houses, Mother struggled to find things to occupy her mind. She had an active social life: bridge parties once a week and occasional luncheons. Her favorite was a reviewers' book club. After reading a book, the reader wrote a review and read it to all the ladies at their monthly meeting, recommending it or not. Some of the ladies found this a great advantage because they didn't have to read the book. They met in each other's homes and, following the program, enjoyed refreshments and conversation.

Daddy never complained about her cooking or housekeeping—neither was up to his mother's standards and my mother knew it. He never complained about anything. He worked long hours at Vorbeck's Sporting Goods—the family business—six, sometimes seven days a week. Back then, he hadn't been promoted to partner yet, but he worked at the store and traveled as a salesman for their wholesale side of the business. When he could, he enjoyed going fishing, attending ball games, and playing poker with his pals. Mother's social life with him included a night out at the picture show and cocktail parties with friends several times a month. Together they attended local plays and traveling musical shows—including the symphony when it came to town.

She wondered in her letters why too often she would rather stay at home with a good book. The symphony moved her—and church. She had left the Presbyterian Church because she liked the Congregational minister's well-articulated sermons better. She was afraid to discuss the emptiness she felt with her husband or even Audra, her closest friend. It was lonely to think that she would only find the answers to her questions in books.

Mother had always loved to write letters and could spend half a day banging away on the old typewriter that had belonged to her father-in-law. Her earlier letters were written in pencil or pen on the backs of envelopes or any other scrap of paper she had handy. She didn't just write to her mother, she composed her letters with detailed descriptions and little scenes, quite masterfully retelling events and conversations complete with quotation marks, sometimes taking hours. By the time her letter was signed it looked a mess, with editing marks, cross-outs, hand-written corrections, and last minute thoughts added on the margins. She enjoyed the whole process so much that she wondered if she could become a writer. With all that joy came the nagging reality that she still had to do the breakfast dishes, make the beds, and get her children bathed or dressed or both or do the washing or marketing and the cooking and ironing. Like most women, she never had a day to herself.

Before they were married, my father said he wanted to be a writer. That attracted her—being married to a writer. She longed to think and talk about important things with her husband. She wanted to learn—to know the truth about *all* things. With all her heart she believed that was possible.

In a detailed account of a pivotal conversation she had with my father one night, she wrote the following to her mother.

> When we got in bed we talked and talked...At last, I got Miles to say he would start to write again...and he did admit that he had always wanted to do just that as a hobby. I think he is going to enter a short story contest in the Salt Lake Paper...I have the dope on it. Oh, Mother, this is what I have been working for [these] four years. I know Miles can write and will if I just keep after him and show him he can find time. We are going to read together and tell each other our thoughts on different subjects, in that way both our minds will be stimulated. Today I am going to get us to promise that we will set two nights apart in each week for just that, and we can go to the store and write and write...I know he can, and perhaps he can teach me the things he knows. All Miles needs is the time, all I need is the technique! Do I deserve so much? I am united with my husband in body, and soul and now to find the thoughts that hide in the far corners of his brain and become united with his mind...It seems natural that the ones I love should share my thoughts. That's why I want Miles' and my minds united in marriage too...I tell you my thoughts because I want you to understand what I think and why I want more than just the "everyday" thoughts. Mother, I can't put my finger on just want it is that I expect from life, but I am sure...that it is nothing that you can measure in $$ and ¢¢...I think [it is an] understanding of people and things. I have many things to learn and in each new thing I find a thrill in it being mine.

Five years had gone by since that late night conversation. Did Mother get some books from the library for them to read aloud? I imagine she did. Did Daddy's lack of passion for the books she brought home erode Mother's hope? They were so far apart in their interests and their levels of curiosity. I see her hope for a more perfect union with her husband as naive. By the time we moved to the country, she was more realistic. By then she was reading psychology, had found an art teacher, and was looking forward to learning how to paint. My father had been promoted, had a larger salary, and enjoyed his work. They had entered their separate worlds.

Two or three times a week, while an assortment of young women babysat for us during the day, Mother disappeared from the house with Verona. They made day trips to blossoming orchards, fields and meadows, and mountain lakes where Verona taught her to paint. At last she had discovered a way to practice a discipline that would make her an artist. With the stimulating philosophies she found in books and visions of oil paintings tugging at her mind every day, she fled from her husband and daughters into the world where she belonged. The charcoal or brush in her hand responded to her will. Her husband and children did not.

My father and grandfather decided that they'd had enough of the retail sporting goods business. They had no patience with customers like the women who came into the store, looked over their rack full of swimsuits, and asked, "Don't you have anything but black?" Black was the traditional color of the modern swimsuit and black, by god, was the only color they were going to carry.

They sold their store on Main Street and moved a couple blocks away to a large four-story building on Fourth Street. There they would expand their business to wholesale only, selling to other sporting goods stores, regional schools, and Mesa College. There was room enough on the first floor for their offices, a warehouse, and a shipping room with a few store fronts leftover to rent. The top stories were rented out as office space.

At home after work, Daddy buried his head in the newspaper and dulled his senses with drink—just like his father. I heard no cross words or arguments, only a tangible silence and vague awareness that nothing was real.

The new building had plenty of room on the fourth floor for my mother to set up a studio. Who knows how hard she had to negotiate with my father for a room with tall windows and a northern exposure? As far as my grandmother was concerned, Bette's new studio was an alarming intrusion into all our lives. She knew that a space of her own meant she had stopped dabbling and had become serious about painting. What kind of woman would turn in her housedresses for slacks and paint-splattered shirts? What kind of mother would leave her children with babysitters during the day while she went into town to paint? Besides, she could not admire Bette's work. The thick brush-strokes, the layering of color, the impressionism, disturbed her. But I admired my mother's work. Especially her landscape of Pinyon Mesa burning with the pink and amber of the sunset and her peach orchard in full bloom against the lush green of a watered desert.

*   *   *

During that long first summer in our new home, my parents were busy with work—my father at the family business and my distracted mother around the house planning the renovation to come. All my friends lived in town. I played with Susan and Gretchen, both of whom had found friends their age on our hill.

We had neighbors I could visit. A farmer and his wife lived just down the lane. Though they looked very old and frail, they kept a cow and chickens, fields of corn and hay, and a large produce garden. When I asked, they would let me follow them around the fields, the garden, the kitchen, and the barn as they did their chores, patiently answering my questions. I loved watching the old farmer irrigate his vegetable garden. He had built a wooden gate that let water run from the main ditch and spill into trenches he hoed between each planted row. How omniscient he seemed as he controlled the flow of water with his shovel, mounding soil into little dams, re-routing the slow trickle of water on to the next row watering the tomatoes, squash, and peppers growing on friable mounds of sandy earth—islands among his gentle rivers.

I tried to talk with him, but the answers to my questions came in very few words and never led to conversation. He never asked me questions about myself and wasn't very friendly. I guessed he was like my father—not very conversational.

One day, after watching him milk the cow, I followed him out past the chicken coop. His tabby cat had given birth to a nest full of kittens behind an old bale of hay. Enthralled by the tiny new babies, I stood by in horror as he removed them one by one from their mother, laid them down in the dust, and chopped off their heads with his miraculous shovel.

"May I—please stop! May I have a kitten?" I desperately hoped to save one. He hadn't even given me time to look at them.

"Too young. Can't be without their mother," he said, lopping off the last head.

All were dead and the mother cat circled the pile of bodies meowing. Horror-struck, I wondered why the mother didn't yowl and tear at his legs with her claws? Why hadn't she leapt up and scratched his eyes out?

I decided that no matter how bored I was I wouldn't go near that farmer again.

Our closest neighbors were Will and Ruth Helgerson. They lived in a small white frame bungalow with a mulberry tree shading the front walk and had two children close to Gretchen's age. While my little sister played with Mrs. Helgerson's children, Susan and I loved helping our stylish neighbor around the house.

Prematurely salt-and-pepper gray, Ruth dressed her slim body to the nines even though she wasn't going anywhere. Mother wore shorts and slacks around the house and didn't dress until she went into town. We seldom saw Ruth without a smoldering Pall Mall in her right hand and a tall glass of strong black iced coffee in the other. Ruth delighted in our company and heaped us with thanks and lavish praise. She told everyone about the adorable girls next door who'd just moved to the country and loved to help her clean.

To Mother, housework was a curse, but Ruth made it fun just by being jolly and offering praise. Only once did Mother make it fun, when she appeared to us dressed as a witch—an old black coat draped over her shoulders and long black gloves. Cackling wildly, she gave her orders and said, "I'll roast you for supper if your work isn't perfect!" We laughed at her joke and cleaned with glee, carrying on the drama with furtive glances over our shoulders. Was the witch watching? And the clock. We'd been given two hours. When it was time for inspection she trailed her black-gloved fingers over the table tops and the book shelves looking for dust. We held our breaths.

We passed the test. For a treat, she cut up two ripe cantaloupes, scooped the seeds out of each half, and filled the hollows with vanilla ice cream. We sat down at the kitchen table and proudly looked around at the order and cleanliness we had created. We asked Mother if next Saturday she would act the witch. I don't remember her answer, but when cleaning day came around again and again, she refused, told us to get to work, and disappeared.

One morning Susan and I arrived early at the Helgerson's. Ruth welcomed us at the kitchen door. "You're going to have to wait a minute while I put on my face."

"Can we watch?"

We followed her to the bathroom door. Reflected in the bright light over the mirror, Ruth's face was almost unrecognizable. Her skin was blotchy and pale, and she had no eyebrows. She draped a towel over her blouse to protect it from spills.

"My mother says I can wear makeup when I am sixteen."

"Sweet sixteen. Well, then you'd better pay attention, and I'll teach you some tricks because that mother of yours doesn't wear makeup."

"She wears lipstick and mascara," Susan reminded.

"First I put on the makeup—this kind is liquid." Ruth tipped a flesh-colored bottle over her finger. Tittering through her teeth, her eyes merry, she dotted her forehead, cheeks, nose, and chin with little dabs of flesh pink then smoothed her face into a blank canvas. "Next, I powder everything down so I won't be shiny." Giggling with delight, she picked up her powder puff and touched it to a compact caked with flesh-colored powder. Then she dusted the surface of her skin. "And now for the eyebrows." Lifting a dark gray pencil, she drew perfect, thinly arched brows.

"Why do you do that? Mother just plucks them." I hoped Ruth wouldn't mind a suggestion.

"Well, my eyebrows aren't naturally pretty like Bette's, so I have to shave them off and paint nice ones on instead." As if this predicament gave her enormous pleasure, she flashed a big smile at the mirror. She curled her eyelashes with an eyelash curler, applied a thick layer of mascara, and painted her lips a shiny red. Dipping her fingers into a pot of rouge, she applied it to her cheeks, the ridge of her nose, and, very softly, under her eyebrows. "That's to give your face a rosy glow," she said, giving her image in the mirror a look of approval. "How do I look?"

"You look beautiful!" And she did.

*   *   *

At eleven, I was a skinny kid with large hazel eyes and what I thought was a gigantic nose. When I looked at my face in the mirror I worried that my pretty days were over. Mother wasn't worried. "You will grow into your face," she said rolling my fine light brown hair into rag curls.

All the girls wore curls, but before I started sixth grade at my new school Mother cut my hair short with straight bangs. She'd decided that my particular features would look more distinctive if I wore my hair Dutch-girl style. I, the new girl, sulked around school wishing I had a gunnysack to put over my head. I didn't want to be different. At home, I whined and begged for curls until Mother finally gave in.

"Don't you want to be an individual?" she asked hotly as she grabbed a lock of my hair. She tied it with a narrow strip of sheet and wound it up into a curl. "Hold still!" she snapped. "Why would you want to be just like everyone else? I don't want you to be ordinary."

"Why would anyone want to be different? Why would anyone want straight hair?"

Mother's hair was straight—pulled flat against her head, tied at the back into a ponytail—just like modern dancer Martha Graham's. Or she'd push it around a doughnut-shaped rat, which made a bun at the nape of her neck. Besides that, she was too different. As part of her drawing exercises she tried to do everything with her left hand and kept dropping things and burning herself. I knew that being different attracted the wrong kind of attention. I'd even heard women say things behind Mother's back. "Bette is lovely, but that hairstyle of hers—so severe, don't you think?" Mother also got suggestions. "Why don't you cut your hair—it's so long and heavy— my hairdresser could give you a perm." Until many years later, I didn't know the history of my mother's desire to be more than "ordinary." She was born plain Betty June Burgess. I'm guessing that after Bette Davis became a big star, Mother changed the spelling of her name to end with an *e* instead of a *y*.

My sisters and I sat down on the thinking bench beside Mother, who held one of her art books open in her lap. I loved her stories about the paintings and the lives of the painters. Every day she gave me an update on the books she was reading. With *Dear Theo: The Autobiography of Vincent Van Gogh,* I listened in earnest and understood how touching Mother found the letters Van Gogh wrote to his brother. But I couldn't comprehend all that grown-up suffering. Most of all I couldn't understand why the artist was hated and rebuffed. I loved his paintings, especially his strange portraits and the picture he painted of the crows flying away in the golden field—symbols of his death to come, Mother said.

I thought Mother read too much. On my way in and out of the house, I saw her lying on the thinking bench reading her books and sensed something wasn't right. I never could have put it into words—even now words are hard—but I felt sorry for her, almost as if she were an invalid who had to force herself to get up just long enough to make lunch and put dinner on the table.

She wanted to read poetry to me—a poem called *Song of Myself.* I could tell by the way she followed me around the house that I would have to listen. Finally, Mother insisted that I sit down and, in her best dramatic voice, read to me.

How creepy, I thought. An old bearded poet talking about atoms, about his tongue and his crotch, and smelling his own breath. And he sounded so conceited. Still, I figured, if Mother admired Walt Whitman, when I grew up I might want to read him. As far as I could tell my mother was odd, but she was also beautiful and intelligent and had good taste in literature, art, and home decoration. Somehow, I also knew how much she loved her daughters.

Before the snows of winter came to Grand Junction, I knew every corner of the land in the country. I had seen the mountains from the top of a cottonwood tree. With my sisters, I'd caught, imprisoned, and played with grasshoppers, water bugs, snakes, lizards, and toads. I knew the soil; the clay hill to the west allowed us to dig a cave and the pale, dry dirt on the road swirled with dust when a car passed by. I knew the sun's settings out the picture window and the sounds of early morning when the rooster crowed and the birds called me awake.

4

Homemaking

1950

"That at present the majority of women neither desire freedom for creative work, nor would know how to use it, is only a sign that we are still living in the shadow of the coercive and dwarfing influences of the past." —Marie Stopes, Married Love, 1918

EVER SINCE CHILDHOOD, when she was trained up in the household arts by her mother, my mother hated housework. Every Saturday Nana Pearl and her girls baked a cake and muffins, stirred and simmered puddings, and cleaned the living rooms. After the baking the kitchen needed scrubbing, sweeping, and mopping until everything sparkled. Her mother made a large dinner for Saturday night. A rib roast or a trio of chickens could be turned into leftovers for Sunday's early dinner after church. Mother and her sister helped Nana with the cooking by stirring pots and peeling vegetables.

The Saturday schedule, along with all five daily schedules, had been honed to perfection by generations of housewives. My mother wanted none of it.

Unless she was giving a party or was expecting guests, our house was usually a mess. When a car crested the hill on the way to our remodeled barn, Mother would shout, "Someone's coming!"

It was time to go into action. Running pell-mell around the living room and kitchen, we piled dirty dishes into the sink, gathered arms full of clothing, magazines, and books, and threw them behind the master bedroom door just as the doorbell rang.

Why did I feel the same utter panic as Mother? I wasn't the homemaker. The visitor wouldn't think less of me. I must have been ashamed for my mother.

None of my friends lived in messy houses. As far as I could tell, other kids' mothers cleaned house every day. I wanted a mother like that. Mother prepared the family meals with the enthusiasm of a prisoner being led to execution. Other mothers had fresh-baked cookies warm out of the oven waiting for their children after school. My usual after school snack was a slice of buttered bread sprinkled with sugar. Ask "what's for dessert" at our house and the answer was, "Nothing." Now and then she bought a box of those little round gingersnaps, so spicy and hard you had to dunk them in milk before you could bite into them.

*   *   *

One summer morning when I was twelve, Mother said, "Before you go for a bike ride, I want you to clean your room—and change your sheets." Mentally checking her list she added, "Then pick up the living room and run the vacuum."

"Can we do it after we get back?"

"Do it now."

"But it'll be all hot in the afternoon."

"Then hurry up and get to work. You'll finish before you know it." Mother was smart enough to know that in the heat of the afternoon my sisters and I would use the same excuse not to clean.

"But Dottie's coming." Dottie was my best friend.

"Dottie can help." She grabbed her purse and headed for the door.

With the cool breeze beckoning from the road, my sisters and I set off to make our beds. We shared the whole second floor, one room that used to be the hayloft.

"Just make your beds," I said to my sisters. "Mother won't notice that we didn't change the sheets."

Mother's car backed out of the carport. We picked up all the dirty clothes and threw them in the closet. It was a long trip to the basement where we did the washing. We closed all the open drawers. Things looked neater that way.

"Dottie's here," Susan said from the window.

We headed downstairs just as Dottie knocked on the kitchen door. I explained what we had to do before we could go.

"Where's your mom?" Dottie looked down the hall toward the master bedroom. Her mother was a good housekeeper.

"She went to her studio." I dragged the vacuum out of the closet and parked it in the middle of the living room thinking we could take a quick ride and be back in time to vacuum before Mother got home. Dottie helped my sisters carry arms full of clutter upstairs to our closet floor, wondering aloud if we would get into trouble. Reassuring her that we would not, I looked around the room and decided it would do.

We took off for a ride in the country, peddling along the road toward the foothills of Mount Garfield. Along the way, we stopped to pick wild sunflowers.

Mother must have decided not to stay long at her studio. Maybe she gave up in frustration. Was she working on a landscape that had failed? Or one of the large drawings we found after her death? The ones on newsprint with India ink and brush, quick strokes of a series of women bound in twisted ropes, their bodies struggling to get free? The ropes were loose and tangled as if the women had accidently gotten mixed up in them. They weren't tied and bound by an abductor, but still troubling enough that we threw them away.

The abandoned vacuum cleaner and the matted shag rug greeted her the moment she entered the house. From the distance of nearly seventy years, I can see her anger mounting as she climbed the stairs to our room, looked around, and opened the closet door. She'd seen this trick before—she'd invented it. Mother took a walk down the hill to the pear thicket and cut herself a long, sturdy switch.

When we girls got home, hungry and thirsty, we found Mother waiting for us behind the screen door. "Send Dottie home," she seethed. I dropped my bike in the dust as Dottie hightailed it. My sisters and I were in trouble and, for some reason, I was completely surprised.

"Come in this house this minute!"

As we started to cross the threshold, Mother grabbed us, one by one, pulled us in, and thrashed the backs of our bare legs. "You deliberately disobeyed me! I looked in your closet. I'll bet you didn't change your sheets. I know you didn't vacuum the living room!"

I was the eldest and expected to lead my little sisters by good example. My head down and tears running down my cheeks, I rubbed the stings on the backs of my legs.

"Now go to your room!" she shouted. Then she added a threat: "Don't come down until your father gets home."

Ignoring the heat, energized by fear, I cleaned out the closet and changed my sheets. My sisters did the same. When the room was clean, we lay down on our beds still panting from the heat. The windows were open, but no breeze drifted in to cool us. There was no relief from the feeling that I deserved the punishment to come. I finally fell asleep. When I woke we watched the clock creep toward seven, the hour our father came home every night after he stopped for cocktails at his mother's.

We gathered near the window and looked out on the lane. "I hope he won't use the hairbrush," Susan whispered.

I looked at my little sisters and felt responsible for the fear in their eyes. "Daddy won't spank you hard. You're younger."

Gretchen shivered, and we drew into a small huddle, arms circling. We sat on the floor leaning against the low windowsill, keeping watch for the first glimpse of his car on the lane, knowing that when he came home there would be "hell to pay." Mother's words.

* * *

He pulled into the carport. The car door slammed. The kitchen door opened. I wiped the tears off my cheeks and listened to the sounds below. The freezer door closed; the ice cube tray banged against the kitchen counter. Footsteps came halfway up the stairs with Mother's voice.

"Your father's home. He wants to see you in the kitchen *right now.*"

Determined not to cry in front of him, I walked slowly down the stairs bracing myself for what would come. Susan and Gretchen followed behind me.

He put his highball down on the table and glared at us. "What do you have to say for yourselves?"

"We're sorry, Mother."

Calm as the eye of a hurricane, he sat down in his chair. "You know what has to happen when you don't mind your mother," he said, looking at us from under his terrifying scowl.

"Yes, Daddy."

"You're first." He was looking at me.

Mother leaned against the kitchen counter with her arms crossed under her breasts, satisfied that justice would be done.

"Please—I promise not to do it again," I whined, knowing it wouldn't make a difference. He wasn't moved. I knew what to do—pull down my panties and place myself bottoms up over his lap. As I fumbled to unbutton my shorts, he said something new.

"Leave your panties on."

I followed through with the rest of the ritual. He spanked me with the hairbrush Mother handed him, raising and lowering it faster and faster as his anger soared and I screamed and cried for him to stop. How did he go from calm to that startling anger? Now I wonder if part of it came from his sense of duty, having to bear the rod like generations of fathers before him.

Unable to stand the sight of my sisters under his blows, I ran back to our room and hid my head under my pillow blocking the sound of their cries. I had always known that no matter how much I wanted to be good, I wasn't. It was not that I hadn't been taught. I was just born bad.

My last spanking would come two years later, when I was fourteen.

* * *

Mother hired Mrs. Nellie Ryan to do housework and laundry and to be an adult presence while she was away at her studio. A large woman with an air of seriousness and dignity, she came to work in a flowered housedress and apron smelling of soap and bacon grease. She parted her gray hair in the middle and wore it flat against her head and gathered into a knot at the nape of her neck. Though she was in her mid-sixties, her face looked pleasantly smooth. Once a week she did the washing in the electric wringer washer down in the basement and hung clothes outside on the umbrella clothesline; while they dried she dusted and ran the vacuum. Sometimes she cooked dinner. Mrs. Ryan returned on another day each week to do the ironing.

I liked to visit with her while she worked. She was not at all like my mother. When I tried to tell Mother my problems (mostly things happening at school), she grew impatient, as if it were a waste of time listening to my nonsense. In the face of her unhappy marriage, her blossoming intellect, and her desperation to run to her studio to paint, my problems must have seemed petty and small. But Mrs. Ryan listened quietly, shaking her head in sympathy. My mother was a flurry of emotion and tension, but Nellie Ryan was as calm as an afternoon cup of tea.

Down in the basement while Mrs. Ryan ironed, Susan embroidered and I stitched a sleeveless blouse on the old pedal Singer sewing machine. Both Mrs. Ryan and my sister were naturally quiet people so it was up to me to deliver the conversation. When I talked about the skin tests I had for my asthma and the allergy shots I got once a week, Mrs. Ryan looked dizzy and said, "What are they gonna think of next?"

I told her about the movies I'd seen and parties I'd attended with my girlfriends. I showed her the large scrapbook I'd started in sixth grade, full of ticket stubs, matchbooks, newspaper stories, photographs and programs from church and school. I showed her the reading certificate I'd received for reading the required seven books. I didn't tell her that I had cheated by reading just enough to fake seven mediocre book reports. When I sang to her, she would smile and nod a pleasant approval. Sometimes she rolled her eyes in dismay at my attempts to amuse her. I asked her questions about her life, but she didn't tell me much, leaving me to wonder if she preferred silence.

Dipping her hand into a bowl of warm water, Mrs. Ryan sprinkled the clothes. Once she had the clothes moistened, she rolled them into a ball. As she worked, her deeply quiet face gave no clue to her thoughts. Except for a faint weariness, her face showed no complaint, no self-pity, no anger toward the husband who had died and left her to work in our basement. I loved to watch her iron, flattening the collar of a starched shirt or skillfully pressing a puffed sleeve as steam and the scent of soap wafted into the air. Mrs. Ryan boiled up starch in the kitchen for my father's shirts and our cotton dresses. She hand-fed the wet clothes into the wringer. The garment, swallowed whole by the rollers, fell into a waiting basket flat and dry as a piece of week-old road kill. I wanted to try everything, but most of all I wanted to run the clothes through the wringer. But first, I had to listen to Mrs. Ryan's cautionary tale.

"My friend, Tillie," she began, "she lives up in Fruita and she sure has a newfound respect for her washing machine. Your mother would never speak to me again if you ended up like her."

I was all ears.

"One day Tillie was doing her wash," she said, fishing around in the washer for a wet piece of clothing. "And she had plenty on her mind. She didn't pay no attention to what was going on, didn't keep her eyes on that wringer. See how I'm catching a little edge first so the wringer takes ahold and the rest can follow?" She was showing me how. "Now you pay attention, so what happened to Tillie won't happen to you."

"Can I try now?"

"First let me finish my story. Well, poor old Tillie. The wringer swallowed up her fingers, then her hand and wrist, then her whole arm went under the rollers and she was trapped there with the wringer going round and round just a gnawing away at her flesh."

"How awful!" I said, shivering at the thought of poor Tillie's arm trapped inside the heartless grip of a machine. "How did she get out?"

"Well, Tillie started up screaming and one of her daughters came a running and unplugged that machine. Then she run and got her daddy out of his orchard. He had to get out his tools and take the wringer apart. To this day Tillie ain't got much but a bone for an arm."

"Poor woman," I said, trying to imagine how that would look in a sleeveless blouse.

After my lesson she let me help her now and then, but she always watched and reminded me of poor Tillie.

Mrs. Ryan had a simple son, Chuck. He had a long white scar on his neck where a goiter had been removed. You could see him around town riding his bike, hunched over peddling with exaggerated effort, his baseball cap perched on the back of his head, dressed too warm for summer.

The Ryans lived way out in the country. I went inside Mrs. Ryan's house only once—to spare the poor woman the embarrassment I imagined she felt when I saw how she lived. Her house was no more than a hole in the ground, a basement. Instead of a house on top, a corrugated piece of tin had been placed over the hole. Mr. Ryan had been building his wife a house when he died. The basement was as far as he got. In their one large room, I saw a kitchen sink and a bare light bulb hanging over an old stove. The room was filled with hundreds of dusty old things settled on shelves, on tables, on the floor: old kitchen implements, canning jars, bicycle parts, hubcaps, wagon wheels, and rusty farm implements. I wonder now if Mrs. Ryan and Chuck were peddlers, trading and selling junk where they could.

I didn't want to think about Mrs. Ryan's circumstances. "Mrs. Ryan's poor, isn't she?"

"Yes, very," my mother answered. I know she gave her hand-me-down clothes, pieces of fabric, anything that we no longer used. Sometimes she drove her into town to the grocery store or to the doctor. When we moved to California she worried aloud about Mrs. Ryan and who would look after her. And when I asked, "What do you miss about Grand Junction?" Mother always said, "Mrs. Ryan."

5

No Joke

1951

OURS WAS NOT a quiet, restful home. Mother, my sisters, and I yelled from room to room and floor to floor, and sometimes we bickered and quarreled. I sang and danced to Broadway show records with the hi-fi woofers and tweeters going full blast. Mother's *The Damnation of Faust* by Hector Berlioz rattled the windows, moving me to wild dance interpretations learned in modern dance class.

Mother approved of our love of music and dance and made sure we took lessons. I studied voice and Susan played the piano. I began piano, but after a year of lessons my piano teacher asked Mother to save her money and not waste his time. Our quiet father found peace inside the bottle and outside working around the property with his best friend, George, the dog.

The depth of Mother's frustration with her life was frequently on full display. From behind a willow switch or a mouthful of loud complaints, her anger was easy to see.

"Why do you torture me like this?"

We'd become so accustomed to the sound of her outrage that she had to turn the volume up louder and louder just to get us to listen.

More than once our mother spoke of her remorse. "Every night before I fall asleep," she said, "I vow to myself that tomorrow I won't scream at you girls—that I'll keep my temper. But I always fail." I know now that we were truly disobedient and wild. The memory of Mother's curse still makes me laugh. "I hope you have three children just like you!"

Especially in summer—with or without permission—we disappeared from the house except for meals and came home long after dark. We swam in the irrigation canal, played softball and night games, like our version of kick the can, with neighborhood kids. We had our own pony and later a horse. We slept in our pasture or at a place we called Bunker Hill far across a neighbor's field, our horses grazing nearby. During our camp-outs we built fires, cooked our supper and breakfast, rolled out our sleeping bags, and fell asleep under the stars.

My father seldom gave advice or entered into family discussions. He seemed inattentive to my mother's editorials on the saving grace of modernism, how the world was supposed to be and wasn't, or the condition of our minds. He seemed uninterested in me. But he must have noticed me sometimes because I cannot forget his eyes zeroing in on me and his terrifying frown. I stepped carefully around him, afraid to make him angry. If I had my hair in pin-curls and didn't look pretty, he looked at me as if he wanted to vomit. Sometimes he would hug my shoulder or pat me on the fanny like sports players do, but I remember most his silence and his remoteness.

None of us knew of Daddy was an alcoholic. He went to work every day and earned a good living, and he was responsible, decent, and well thought of in the community. He never looked or acted drunk.

His favorite actor was W.C. Fields, who always played drunks in the movies. Daddy took me to see a matinee of one of his twenty-year-old films. The theater was almost empty, but he wanted to sit close to the screen. I had never known my father to give in to laughter. He smiled now and then, or chuckled, but unrestrained laughter was uncommon. During the film his almost hysterical hilarity truly frightened me as I looked up at the screen and cringed beneath the giant black and white intoxicated clown.

My mother's passion for art and literature matched my father's passion for work. They had no passion for each other, but we didn't know that. We thought our behavior caused all the currents of unhappiness in the house. Our mother yelled at us, not at our father. The two of them never fought. No storm clouds rolled over the murky skies, no thunder and lightning lit up the atmosphere, no rain fell to clear the dust from the air. We children had nothing to name, no visible signs that something was terribly wrong. We believed that those long, discomfited silences were our fault.

No matter the tortures of her day, Mother came to tuck us in and kiss us goodnight. Sometimes, especially as I grew older, I didn't want her kiss. I couldn't stand for her to touch me. But I never pushed her away or turned my back on her. Deep inside, I felt sorry for her.

*   *   *

Meals were served in the small kitchen at a round oak pedestal table. Mother sat nearest the stove, then Daddy, then the daughters, ranked by age, on colorful stools my mother had rubbed with a rainbow of pigments. Stools fit our style of dining better than chairs.

Mother almost never cooked enough to fill me up. She didn't seem to know how much food three growing children and one adult male would eat. Still hungry after dinner, sometimes we passed a loaf of bread and jars of peanut butter and jelly. While we filled up, she'd pour herself a cup of coffee and light up. She'd pull smoke into her lungs, sip her thick black coffee, and disappear somewhere inside her head. Mother didn't care about food. She had no real appetite to drive her to the kitchen. How to cook a perfect roast beef was not her question.

Mealtimes were just another time for our father to correct the children.

"Sit up straight, Karen! You'll get a hunchback."

I straightened my back and picked up my fork.

"Put your napkin in your lap."

I put my napkin in my lap.

Besides table manners, he was also an expert on social decorum and proper English. He never allowed singing at the table—not even the new song I learned from my voice teacher. I knew not to be excitable in any way at the table. Sometimes after we began on such-and-such a topic, we heard, "You don't talk about that at the dinner table!"

"You haven't finished your liver, Susan."

"Can I have some ketchup?'

"No! That's an insult to the cook."

"At least it's not tongue," I said, trying to see the bright side. I liked my mother's boiled tongue dinner, but Susan could barely choke it down. I shook the bottle of Kraft's French dressing and dribbled it over the iceberg lettuce salad lying on my plate next to the greasy fried potatoes. I was always hungry and would even eat my mother's boiled-to-death vegetables swimming in melted margarine.

"Knock, knock," I said, trying to chase away the dinnertime gloom.

"Who's there?" Gretchen asked.

"Isadore."

"Isadore who?"

"Isadore locked? I can't get in."

My sisters roared, nearly falling off their stools.

And then silence.

As an uncomfortable hush settled like a thick fog over our table, we went back to our food. I couldn't stand the silence. "Guess what I saw on the way to school this morning? You'll never guess—right in the middle of the road—the biggest snake you've ever seen. It looked like a boa constrictor—but it was dead—flat as a pancake—like someone had run over it ten times on purpose."

"Don't talk about things like that while we're eating."

I took a deep breath and changed the subject. "At school today I noticed the funniest thing—the blackboards are green—get it? Green blackboards! I think that's silly. Blackboards should be black—I wonder what genius decided to make them green? We should call them greenboards from now on," I laughed, rolling my eyes, tipping precariously onto two legs of my stool. "What color were your blackboards, Daddy?"

"Black."

And the fog settled in.

"Dottie was absent from school today. When I called her after school she said she had a cold—hope I don't get it—some other kids have it too—if I get it then you'll probably, most likely, almost certainly get it too—"

"For god's sake, will you be quiet," Daddy barked. "You sound like you've been vaccinated with a phonograph needle!" His anger had traced its way to his dark eyes and turned his brow into a deep canyon, but his words sounded so funny that I got the giggles.

Vaccinated with a phonograph needle! I couldn't help it. I tried to swallow the laughter that erupted like a sneezing fit. "That's so funny, Daddy," I gasped, trying to stifle myself.

My father teetered on the brink of rage, but thank God my mother and sisters laughed too. Our giggles could not be suppressed. We rejoiced as Daddy's resolve crumbled and he got the giggles too. Though the chore was always perilous, sometimes I could change the mood at our table.

That evening, my father decided to ask us a riddle. "Why do cows wear bells?"

None of us could guess.

"Because their horns don't work."

"I don't get it," I said.

"Horns, knucklehead," he sounded disappointed. "Honk! Honk!"

"I still don't get it."

"Then just give him a courtesy laugh," Mother scolded.

"Polite young ladies laugh when someone tells a joke," my father said. And the gloom descended once more.

*   *   *

The dream never varied. In dark immeasurable space a huge globe spiraled high above me. My terror built as its orbit whirled it closer and closer until it hit me repeatedly on the head. It wasn't pain that terrified me, but the globe's haunting—the presence I could not escape no matter where I tried to hide. I'd leap out of bed and crawl across the floor in my sleep. Once I woke up and found myself on my hands and knees trying to crawl head-first down the stairs. After a while I was afraid to go to sleep. I described the dream to my mother. She looked worried and tried to reassure me. After a couple of weeks with no relief, I plagued her about the dream. I needed to know what it meant. I needed her to lie down beside me until I fell asleep. But I didn't know how to ask.

She decided to help by making Susan sleep with me. Tucking us in for the night, she kissed our foreheads, and after saying, "Close your eyes and go to sleep," left my nine-year-old sister to protect me.

Side-by-side in the dark, Susan took my hand. "You're okay," she whispered. "Now go to sleep." Snuggled against her, I let myself relax and fell asleep.

By the middle of the night I was screaming. Susan sat up terrified as I jumped up from under the covers and flew out of bed, spinning in my long nightgown, my head thrown back, my arms held out like wings. "But I'm alive. I'm alive!" I howled, crumbling to the floor. I got up on my hands and knees and crawled frantically across the dark floor toward my only escape—the stairs. I scared Susan so badly that she begged our mother not to make her sleep with me again.

* * *

One day I could not breathe, and my worried mother called Dr. Graves. He had come to the house many times before, driving up our country lane in his shiny black sedan, wearing his dark suit, white starched shirt, and tie stuck with a big diamond. I thought he was the handsomest man in Grand Junction. Usually I waited at the window, watching as he took his black bag off the back seat. But the day my lungs failed me I could not run to the window. My mother made me lie down on the thinking bench, where I struggled for every breath.

Dr. Graves came into the room smiling, but the moment he saw me he knelt on the floor beside me, a look of profound concern on his face.

"You don't look so good, honey child," he said, placing a big warm hand on my solar plexus. "I've got something here that will fix you right up." He searched my face. "You don't have to say a word, kid. Just try to relax."

I loved Dr. Graves. His handsome, sympathetic face said he cared for me too. As his eyes probed for clues to my condition, his warm hand melted my fear away. He reached into his bag, loaded up the syringe, and gave me a shot of adrenaline.

"You're gonna feel like your engine's been turned up to high now, honey," he said, as I grabbed his hand. "Just two shakes of a lamb's tail and you'll be just fine." Almost immediately my heart began to race. In moments my lungs opened. I could breathe. "See, what'd I tell ya! Has Dr. Graves ever told you a lie?"

Never, I thought, shaking my head no, helping myself to a big breath of air.

He diagnosed asthma. My grandparents paid for visits to an allergist and years of allergy shots. Still, for many years, there were trips to the emergency room. People wondered what kind of psychological stress I suffered.

"I'm fine," I assured, "just allergic to the pollens of grasses and trees and the dust off moths' wings." I thought that made me sound so interesting, so out of the ordinary. Maybe a little bit like that truly unique individual my mother wanted me to be.

Bette, Karen, and Herman "Miles" Vorbeck, 1938

Downtown Grand Junction, CO, early 1950s

Karen at Redstone Barn Dance, 1950

Karen modeling haute couture, Catalina Island, 1957

Karen as Queen of the Sadie Hawkins Day dance, 1953

GIFTS FOR NIXONS are given by three-year-old Priscilla Bowman and Karen Verbeck. Priscilla presented Senator Nixon, vice presidential candidate on the Republican ticket, with a Palisade peach, and a corsage, which Mrs. Nixon is holding, along with a bouquet which was also presented to her.—Daily Sentinel photo.

Fun Day '51

ESTERN UNI
TELEGRAM

JUNCTION COLO 22 600P MST

6 PHONE CL89316 SAN JOSE CALIF
FRANCISCO JANUARY FIRST 225PM

Mesa County
School District
REPO
of Pupil's
Junior-Senior
GRAND JUNCTION
REPORT
Grade
JUNIOR SENIOR HIGH
Junior High

A page from Karen's scrapbook, early 1950s

Karen as peasant girl in Camille,
Catalina Players, 1957

Karen, waiting for Jim on their
wedding day, 1959

Karen's first stage appearance in Wind from the Sea, Ojai Arts Center, 1955

Karen's engagement photo for
newspaper announcements, 1959

Karen in Maria Marten or
Murder in the Old Stone Barn,
Catalina Players, 1957

6

Best Friends

1951

PEGGY ANN LIVED a quarter mile away from our house on her family's farm in a sprawling white farmhouse with a big front porch and an old red barn out back. Her angel face, spun gold hair and round body reminded me of the pretty dolls Santa used to leave under our Christmas tree.

Another half-mile down the road and we were at Dottie's, a small run-down house standing alone alongside the road. She was long-legged and tall as a boy. Wavy brown hair, big brown eyes, and lips with perfect twin peaks.

Before the end of seventh grade Peggy Ann, Dottie, and I called ourselves the Three Musketeers.

Peggy Ann had a marvelously adventurous spirit, and when we put our heads together we came up with all kinds of fun. But no matter what the three of us decided to do, Dottie's first thought was whether or not we'd get into trouble. *Would this please my parents?* was her question. I knew that no matter what, I wasn't going to please mine, and Peggy Ann figured that what her parents didn't know wouldn't hurt them. Much to her detriment Dottie carried this little rulebook around in her head making her very easy to shock. Peggy Ann and I soon perfected the sport of making the poor girl's eyes pop.

Because all our other girlfriends lived in town and we seldom got to see them, the summer between seventh and eighth grade I woke up each morning eager for adventure with Dottie and Peggy Ann. We had all of outdoors to explore and horses to ride. Often we swam in the canal which wandered just a short walk down our lane across First Street.

Grand Junction's canals crisscrossed the desert valley, bringing river water to the orchards and fields and turning the land into a farming paradise. Nine hundred thousand peach trees transformed the valley into a blossoming fairyland in spring.

One day, tucked in our inner tubes, we floated downstream a long distance, stranding ourselves in the middle of some farmer's field. We were forced to crawl out of the canal and walk home on the hot asphalt road, hopping on one bare foot or the other or alongside the road through stickers and tumbleweeds.

The wooden bridges that crossed the canal were almost road level with silty water the color of chocolate milk floating only a foot or so below the bridge. We often had a destination in mind that led us downstream to a second bridge. Drifting under the bridges, spiders' webs dangled above our heads and tangled in our hair. We weren't stopped because we knew our wildlife. We jarred them, poked at them, and stared them in the face with fascination. If they weren't black widows or scorpions, they were not that fearsome.

For excitement, we climbed the stepping boards nailed to a tall cottonwood on the canal bank. Grabbing a long rope, we'd swing out over the slow-moving water, flying, letting go for a heart-pounding plunge.

We took long bike rides together, sometimes riding three miles into town. One of our favorite destinations was Vick's Pastry Shop on Main Street—the second best show in town. The first was Pantuso's Shoe Store, where they had a miraculous x-ray machine. You could x-ray your feet to see if your new shoes would fit. Even when we weren't buying shoes, we'd stop by and watch our toe bones wiggle. We couldn't look at our bones too often or Mr. Pantuso would ask us to leave.

Through the pastry shop's large plate-glass window, we could watch the doughnut machine plop perfect rings of dough onto the conveyor belt and float them off into a vat of boiling oil. As the doughnuts sizzled and swam, the delicious smell of frying dough drifted out to the street. The machine flipped the doughnuts, gently bobbed them one-by-one out of the oil, and tumbled them golden brown into an outgoing basket.

The first thing we saw when we walked through Vick's door was the display case. Front and center: a tray full of fat cream puffs. I always got a cream puff, but first I had to feast my eyes on the gallery of decorated cakes posing on white paper doilies, glossy-topped apple pies, sticky buns, and spongy white bread. The lady behind the counter wore a pink uniform with a ruffled white apron, and a pointed cap stuck to her head with bobby pins. We stood on the sidewalk straddling our bikes, devouring cream puffs, dropping a blizzard of powdered sugar on our blouses and shoes. We rode home thirsty as tumbleweeds, stopping for lemonade at Dottie's.

Riding north toward my house, we got off our bikes again to pick sunflowers just below the hill. That's when Dottie got us into a philosophical discussion.

"You gotta be ready," she said, "You never know when you're gonna die. If you die just after you commit a sin, you'll go straight to hell."

"I don't believe that," I said.

"Me neither," Peggy agreed. "Besides, we don't die until God says your number's up."

"You mean you could stand right here in the middle of the road and if it ain't your time a car won't hit you?" Dottie asked.

"Don't say 'ain't,'" she corrected gently. "But that's right, no matter how careful you are, if God wants you then you're finished."

Looking seriously thoughtful, Dottie pursed her mouth and rolled her eyes toward the sky. She didn't look convinced.

I don't remember who dared whom to lie down on the double yellow line in the middle of First Street, but both Peggy Ann and I let our bikes fall in the weeds and lay down head to toe.

"Dare you, Dots! Double-dare you!"

Dottie, her eyes wide—as if she'd never seen anything so asinine before—flatly refused. "No! Are you nuts? Jeez, if a car comes fast over that hill it'll smash you flat as pancakes!"

As we lay spread-eagle in the middle of the road we didn't consider that Dottie could be right. We were brave and trusting in God's goodness and wisdom while Dottie wasn't. Though she looked frantic and bewildered, I thought I could see admiration for us in her eyes.

"I think you're both crazy!" she yelled, running to the top of the hill to watch for cars.

I could tell that she wished she was brave.

"If you don't get up right this minute," she hollered, "I'm going home!"

We didn't move.

"I'm not gonna stand here and watch you get killed," she screeched, stomping off to her bicycle. She rode away, leaving the scene of the accident before it happened.

Peggy Ann and I stayed there on the double yellow line for what seemed like an hour, listening for the sound of a car barreling south toward the spot where we lay spread-eagle. But no cars came. I was bored, and cloud watching was out of the question. The sky was clear and blue. There was nothing to see except a couple of hawks circling lower and lower. Maybe they thought we were road-kill. After a while the road felt hard and hot as—well—asphalt, and lying there in the sun got more and more boring. We decided we'd get up and go for a ride down to Dottie's.

When we knocked on Dottie's door she looked happy to see us alive. She welcomed us inside with, "Wanna make fudge?"

Usually when we went to Dottie's house we brought our embroidery to occupy our hands while we listened to the hit parade on the radio. We embroidered from store-bought patterns of butterflies, flowers, birds, and the like, ironed on pillow cases, handkerchiefs, and tea towels. When they were finished we hid them away to give as Christmas presents. By then I knew that mother would have nothing to do with an embroidered cloth doily, so I gave my embroidered works to my grandmothers. Mother went wild with disdain when paint-by-number came into style and if we hadn't begged her to distraction, we never would have had coloring books. Sometimes at Dottie's we'd make fudge or bake a Duncan Hines devil's food cake, smothering it with our own homemade coffee frosting. We were too impatient to wait for the layers to cool so our icing always slid off the cake. It didn't matter how our cakes looked. We ate them right away.

* * *

Peggy's and Dottie's mothers didn't smoke so we stole cigarettes from my mother.

"You're gonna get into big trouble," Dottie said, refusing to light up. "Dang it, you guys! Don't you know that smoking will turn you into midgets!"

"We don't care," Peggy Ann said. Besides, we didn't believe that.

"You sound like one of those people who say, 'Don't frown or your face will freeze.'"

"Or, 'a nail dissolves in a Coke—think what it will do to your stomach.'"

"Well, you can be dumb if you want," Dottie said, "but I believe those things—except about the frown—cigarettes ain't good for you and fooling around with matches is dangerous!"

"We don't care," Peggy Ann said, arching one eyebrow. "And don't say ain't."

One day, when we were bored and really wanted to smoke, we couldn't get cigarettes because my mother had gone out with her pocketbook.

"Let's make some fudge." Dottie bounced to her feet, already on the way into the kitchen.

Peggy Ann and I declined. We weren't in the mood to stand around a hot kitchen waiting for the hard ball stage. We wanted to stay right there, at the base of the cottonwood, and smoke—like grown-ups. To practice our new skills—how to French inhale, blow smoke rings, and like Rita Hayworth, let smoke curl from our sultry lips.

I stripped the dry stringy substance from under the bark of the tree, rolled it in a piece of newspaper, and twisted one end, making a smoke that looked more like a cigar than a cigarette.

"It's so big we can share it," I reasoned, striking a wooden match against the base of the tree. The match flamed, and I put the tree-bark cigarette to my lips and dragged. A huge flame shot into the air. I jumped up off the ground as the stench of burning hair filled the air.

"Is my hair on fire?"

"No," Peggy Ann said inspecting my bangs, "Just singed—and your eyebrows—"

Dottie gasped for words as she rolled around in the grass, laughing and screaming, "I told you so—I told you so!"

* * *

Every Saturday morning year-round, we paid twenty cents to see the picture show at the Cooper Theatre. With the balcony closed, the place filled up with junior high school kids. We sat down with ten-cent bags of popcorn, boxes of Good & Plenty, red wax lips, and candy cigarettes. The red velvet curtain swung open, the lights went down low, and the atmosphere inside the Cooper turned positively electric.

First they showed five or more cartoons, then a newsreel, then a singing cowboy movie starring Gene Autry or Roy Rogers followed by a second feature starring Bud Abbott and Lou Costello or the Three Stooges. I liked Abbot and Costello best. We got up and down to go to the candy counter or changed seats to visit with friends. The movies were just an excuse to swarm together in the dark. We could hardly wait for the magic moment when a boy tapped us on the shoulder and asked to sit with us. That's how I got my first boyfriend.

When he eased into the seat beside me, Billy wasted no time. He grabbed my hand and we sat together in the dark with the light from the screen bouncing off our faces. I couldn't speak or even look at him. I didn't dare acknowledge the excitement happening in our hands, the baffling ecstasy that made my whole body tingle.

* * *

In eighth grade, on the day of our annual Play Day, the girls were allowed to wear pedal pushers to school. On this day alone: no dresses, no homework. Boys and girls would compete side-by-side in track events, races and relays, kickball and softball games. Dottie, Peggy Ann, and I rode our bikes into town.

The school grounds had a baseball field and a track across the street where my relay teammate handed me the baton and I took off, my lungs bursting as I carried the baton to the finish line. In a whirl of dust and the flash and gleam of all those bicycles straining to win, I pumped my bike around tight curves and made it to the finish line *first*. I won two blue ribbons: one for being on the winning relay team and the other for placing first in the bike race. I won two white ribbons for placing third in two other events, giving me more ribbons than anyone of either sex in my eighth grade homeroom. In a little ceremony of recognition, my teacher presented me with the homeroom flag. It would be mine for the night.

That night I showed my family the shiny purple and gold satin flag and all my ribbons. I described all the races and told them how my teacher had honored me in class.

"Boys aren't going to like you if you beat them in sports!" My father looked concerned. "If you keep this up, you'll get muscle-bound. Men don't like muscle-bound women."

My mother agreed. For the same reasons, she had quit gymnastics at about my age.

"But unlike you," she said, "a girl who has never committed herself to anything seriously, I was dedicated to the sport."

She had practiced for years and performed at assemblies. She had been an excellent competitive diver as well, and knew how to swan dive and somersault off the high board. She'd had real athletic ability and had given it all up out of respect for her femininity.

At that very moment, I faced a turning point in my life. Growing up, becoming a lady, meant giving up childish things like sports. I listened to what they had to say, rolled my flag around its pole, and finally put it away.

In a kind of coming-of-age ritual, and with a whole new grown-up outlook on life, I returned the flag to my homeroom. I put aside my joy in climbing trees, softball, biking, and track. I wouldn't participate in sports again. I denied myself any sadness or regret. It was the earliest time that I now remember hiding my feelings from myself—a skill I developed to perfection. I didn't bid "farewell" to my childhood. I didn't feel cheated or oppressed and wondered why on earth I had wanted to cry when my parents weren't thrilled by my Play Day ribbons and flag.

After school the next day, I took off my clothes and looked at my body in the full-length mirror: my small waist above curved hips and my breasts—they were bigger than most of my friends'. It wasn't too late. The reflection of my body revealed no bulging muscles. I had to flex them like a boy showing off before you could even see them. Overnight my hazel eyes and full lips had come to dominate my face, putting my nose into perspective. I was pretty. If I had to be critical, I thought my face was a little too round and that my plain brown hair should be a shining auburn and wavy and maybe longer and certainly more obedient, but I had to admit, I'd turned out pretty.

Luckily, I already knew some of the skills young ladies should know, like how to smile and make small talk in social settings. I knew how to walk gracefully. Dottie, Peggy Ann, and I had practiced with books on our heads. We knew how to tuck our hips under, lift our chins, and glide so the book wouldn't fall off. I knew how important it was to hold in my tummy, though sometimes I forgot and then my mother would remind me.

* * *

On occasion our father took the whole family out to dinner at the Café Caravan, a new, very-fancy-for-Grand-Junction establishment on Main Street. We girls sipped Shirley Temples while watching live parrots and a monkey hop through the tropical foliage behind the bar. In the large aquarium that served as a room divider, brightly colored fish darted in and around the swaying water vines and through the doors and windows of a ceramic castle. We had never seen anything so exotic. In the dining room we listened to the band play, and between bites of fried shrimp, my sisters and I took turns dancing with Daddy.

He had already taught me the steps to the waltz and the foxtrot, and he thought I was ready to learn how to rumba. Along with teaching dance steps, he stressed the importance of carrying on good conversation while I danced.

"You must learn to anticipate your partner's every move." And referring to how my arm hung on his arm and my hand weighted his, he said, "Never let your partner feel your weight."

I had finally become interesting to my father. He had something to teach me. With my best interests in mind, he gave me the information I would need to attract a husband and to be a good wife: never beat a man at games, never let him feel your weight, and anticipate his every move. His most memorable bit of fatherly advice came later: "When naked, never bend over with your back to your husband." I understood him to mean that particular view would be unsightly.

As we danced I remembered to lay my arm lightly on his arm and to rest my hand just barely in his. My father was a good dancer. He knew the steps as he whirled me around the floor. He held me close, humming in my ear, his whiskey breath wafting around my head like a cloud. A feather in his arms, I dipped when he dipped, swayed when he swayed, my feet stepping in time with his. But it wasn't fun. Pleasing my father was hard work.

His eldest daughter was no scholar, maybe she was a knucklehead, but she was beautiful and she could handle herself on the dance floor. He didn't say a word, but I knew how proud he felt partnering me as we danced or as he squired me down the street. And at a Kiwanis Club luncheon I watched him grin from ear to ear as he introduced me to his comrades as, "Karen, the eldest of my three queens."

* * *

The night of the school dance, I brushed my hair into a ponytail and tied it with a ribbon to match my dress. I put on my new garter belt, nylon stockings, and white ballerina-style flats. Dottie wasn't allowed to go to school dances, but our parents took turns driving Peggy Ann and me.

Dancing close in a cute boy's arms, my cheek pressed against his cheek, I remembered everything my father had taught me—except the interesting conversation. That seemed impossible. Talking spoiled the magic—the inebriating feelings that came as we moved to the music. How I smiled or how I touched his hand seemed to affect him. I had some mysterious power over him and I liked the secret power he held over me. And at the end of the dance, when he squeezed my hand, I knew that he liked me and would ask me to dance again. If, by the end of the evening, he had filled in my dance card, I knew he would be my next boyfriend.

7

Redstone

1951

GREEN WITH NAUSEA, our ears popping, my sisters and I sprawled in the back seat as our father steered the navy-blue Mercury around an eternity of hairpin turns. We'd already had miles of singing "You Are my Sunshine" and "Don't Fence Me In" and miles of listening to me passionately sing "Nature Boy" over and over again. I was thirteen, Susan, ten, and Gretchen, seven; we also entertained ourselves by picking little fights with one another.

Mother drew imaginary lines on the back seat to keep us apart. "Susan, you sit here, in the middle. Karen—behind Daddy. Gretchen, scooch over behind me. Now stay in your own places!"

We'd do as she said and there would be peace for a minute, then—

"M-o-o-other! Susan touched me!"

"Tell Karen to get her toe off my side of the seat."

"Make Gretchen stop kicking me!"

Under threat, we'd finally quiet down.

After a hundred miles, most of it on winding mountain roads, I clung to the open window with both hands, resting my cheek on the cold steel door. Eyes closed, inhaling deeply the high mountain air, I hoped my breakfast would stay down.

With the stench from our parents' cigarettes clinging to our clothes, hair, and lungs, we tried to fall asleep. Sleep made the time go faster, but the last ten miles to Redstone seemed interminably long. As we approached the little village below the red rock cliffs, the sound of the Crystal River roaring in the cool pine-fragrant air revived me. My whole body rejoiced in anticipation of seeing once more the most wonderful place on the earth.

Redstone was hidden away in a high valley in the Elk Mountains east of Grand Junction. A single row of white Edwardian cottages and the general store with its one gas pump had been built on one side of the Crystal River. Except for the crumbling ruins of some two-hundred coke ovens, the other side was populated only by aspens and wildflowers.

Our neighbors, Ruth and Will Helgerson, owned the cottage we rented for a month each summer. We had no electricity, but one year they installed indoor plumbing. The front room was dark and uninviting. A coal stove stood against one wall, wilted sheer curtains hung at the windows, and tiny brown and yellow flowers bloomed on the buff-colored wallpaper. The lumpy old davenport waited under the shelf where the kerosene lamps were stored during the day.

The center of our lives at Redstone was the large sunny kitchen with a family-sized table and a big wood stove. In a cast iron skillet, we fried bacon and eggs, trout, and chicken. Proficient enough at fire building, we turned out perfectly respectable cakes and biscuits from the oven. During our first years at Redstone, before the indoor plumbing was installed, a hand pump brought water to the kitchen sink and a galvanized tub set up on the kitchen table served as a bathtub for children. As part of our great adventure, we heated water on the stove, brought in the same galvanized wash tub and the scrubbing board and washed our clothes by hand. Just like our great-grandmothers, we ironed with heavy irons heated on the stove. In those days, no wash and wear fabrics existed and wrinkles were near to scandalous. Every day we children went on a treasure hunt for firewood—mostly kindling. Redstone, the Helgerson's cottage, the mountains, and the river were enchanted for me.

After a week's vacation, our father had to work and would drive up to the village only on weekends. Sometimes we followed him across the road to the Crystal River to watch him fish. He remained devoted to the sport even though he never had much luck. Our attention spans permitted us to watch his search through his large collection of hand-tied flies, his final selection, and the tying of the fly to the line.

"This one's prettier, why did you pick *that* fly?"

"It looks tasty to me."

None of us girls were interested in fishing, but we cooperated by being quiet—not scaring the fish away. For a few minutes we would watch this lonely man wade into the river and cast his line over the water. While we waited for a fish to bite, we collected pretty stones sparkling on the river bottom. When nothing happened, we wandered off down the riverbank, finally scampering off to the general store for Fudgsicles.

*   *   *

The summer after the sixth grade I had been happy to leave Grand Junction and my friends for a month. But by the next summer I wanted to bring a friend. Our parents had agreed that Dottie could come for one week.

I could hardly wait to show Dottie around Redstone, where John Osgood, a wealthy turn-of-the-century-industrialist, had built his utopian village. We lived in one of the little cottages he constructed for the families of the men employed at the coke ovens and mines. I knew Dottie would be impressed with the Dutch-style inn with the high square clock tower built for the bachelors who worked there. And her eyes would pop when she saw the forty-two-room mansion where Osgood lived with his wife, Lady Bountiful. John D. Rockefeller and J.P. Morgan had dined there, and now that it was open to the public, on rare occasions, so did we. Osgood's utopia lasted all of seven years. Then the mines folded and the village was abandoned.

That summer my mother's old high school friend Louise came all the way from Hollywood, California, to visit us in Redstone.

Mother and her friend were as different as Main Street is from Rodeo Drive. Louise bounced out of bed every morning already dolled up, looking like she had just come from a beauty parlor. Her clothes and jewelry looked expensive. She spoke with a careful sweet voice punctuated by a lady-like enunciation of every single syllable. When she laughed, her voice tinkled like a silvery bell. I thought she was divine. Dottie was scared of her.

One afternoon I asked Louise if she would be my partner in a game of Canasta. Susan said, "I want to play too!"

"Great, Susie-Q, *you* be my partner," Louise said, putting her arm around Susan's shoulder like they were best pals.

Trying to be a good sport, I said nothing about the fact that I had asked Louise first. Mother teamed up with me, and Dottie sat out the hand.

All of a sudden my hand was full of pairs and wild cards. As the game progressed I couldn't draw a bad card. I discarded like a psychic and claimed a large discard pile. My game advanced brilliantly as I captured a second and then a third discard pile.

I bet Louise is sorry she's stuck with Susan.

Then Susan picked up the largest discard pile I'd ever seen—the one I had hoped to take on my next turn. My lucky streak was over, and I watched helplessly as my younger sister became the dominant player on their team. When we lost the game, I slammed my hand full of cards on the table, where they flew all over the room like the deck of Wonderland cards in Alice's dream.

"You don't have to be a bad sport, Karen!" Louise sounded shocked.

"Nobody wants to play with a sore loser." Mother looked disappointed.

Susan and Dottie just looked at me like I was a jerk. With tears blinding my eyes I stomped out of the kitchen and ran across the meadow at the back of the house to the trail that headed up the mountain.

Utter embarrassment and rage drove me. It was all so unfair. Sobbing, I tramped up the narrow trail. It seemed so easy for everyone else to be sweet, generous, and thoughtful.

"I'm not a good sport!" I screamed, my voice flushing birds out of the bushes. I had to *pretend* to be gracious when I lost. In a game of cards, or at school when I was put out on home plate, I felt crushed. Most of the time I knew how to overwhelm my feelings, how to act nice, and make people think I wasn't mad, or jealous, or selfish, or mean. *But I'm not nice.* I hated losing, especially to Susan, my too perfect sister.

To keep myself from stumbling over roots and stones on the path I looked down at the trail under foot. As I passed through the forest I could hear the river in the valley below. The previous summer a sheepherder had taken his flock up that same mountain to graze. He camped there for weeks, came down with tick fever, and died.

I hoped I'd get tick fever and lie for days in our dreary little room at the cottage, a white sheet covering my fevered body. With a dish of cool water between them, my mother and Louise would mop my brow. I hoped Dottie and my sisters would weep in the dark hallway and my father would have to tear himself away from work and come back to Redstone. And when the fever consumed me they would pull the white sheet over my tormented face and cry, "We're sorry, Karen, we didn't mean it. You weren't a bad sport—just a poor disappointed girl."

I had been up the trail several times before but never so far. As the trail thinned out, I reassured myself that hunters came that way in search of deer and elk. I found a little creek trickling over smooth shiny rocks and stopped to rest. My mother had told me never to drink from lakes or streams unless I knew the water was safe. I wondered if the water was poison. I didn't care. I knelt down, and making a cup of my hands, took a sip of cool water.

Sitting on a nearby rock to think, I remembered a story I'd heard at Redstone. A cowboy had ridden his horse up a mountain trail— just like this one. Somehow he slipped and fell to his death far below in the creek. They never found his body but years later they found the skeleton of his horse tied to a tree.

As the sun slipped behind the mountain I had to admit that I was scared and hungry. I'd been gone several hours, and thoughts of ticks and wild cats and all the other animals who hunted at night forced me to go home. I would have to face everyone. Bolstered by the face-saving prospect that my mother and Louise were worried, maybe even sorry, I headed back down the mountain trail. For what seemed like a long time I lingered at the edge of the forest waiting for it to get darker—watching the house, hoping that everyone inside had missed me. Maybe they had called over to Carbondale for the police.

Finally I walked through the kitchen door and found everyone gathered around the table—my mother, Louise, Dottie, and my sisters. They had almost finished dinner. No one asked where I'd been or even mentioned that I'd been gone. All I heard was, "You're late for dinner." I'd heard that before.

I dropped into my empty chair next to Dottie, so ashamed I couldn't look at her. My mother handed me the plate she'd kept warm in the oven. While listening to Louise finish the story I had interrupted, I buttered my baked potato and chewed a dried-out bite of hamburger steak. Everyone laughed when she delivered the punch line. They hadn't worried at all. My mother put a big bowl of chocolate pudding on the table and everyone helped themselves.

*   *   *

Sometimes there were things to do in the evening—a party at one of the other cottages, a square dance, or dinner and a concert at the mansion. The parties—always for the adults—included a long cocktail hour, followed by a late dinner, followed by what they called nightcaps or one-for-the-road.

"Before you leave, won't you have one for the road?" they would urge their guests into the wee hours.

While the adults talked and laughed, the kids wandered off to play hide and seek. Sometimes we just went for a walk in the moonlight—no particular destination in mind—greeting people on the road and stopping on front porches to chat with villagers.

My father and other men, both family and friends, were at Redstone the evening Dottie and I left the cottage for a walk toward the inn. In shadows, we passed by the picnic table where my parents entertained a jolly crowd. None of them noticed us. Out of the dark boomed a familiar voice animated by too much liquor.

"Have you looked at Karen lately?" my Uncle Gene's voice resounded, "She's gorgeous! Even a priest would be tempted to rape her. No one would blame him!"

Everyone laughed.

"You hear that?" Dottie asked, as a wave of confusion nearly knocked me off my feet. "He thinks you're really beautiful!"

"I don't think I am!" I blurted, reassuring Dottie that I was not conceited. At thirteen I knew of no greater sin for a girl than conceit.

Uncle Gene had said what people believed. Men raped because they could not resist female beauty or because bad girls lured them to uncontrollable lust. No one I knew spoke of priests and sex in the same breath. The idea seemed fantastic. Flattered at some level, and frightened that I might have evil powers over men, I wandered down the road with Dottie at my side. My head swam in the light of the full moon, wondering if men were watching as I passed and if they had thoughts of leaping out of the dark underbrush to ravish me.

* * *

We stayed in the cottage at night and played cards or told ghost stories. After fighting over whose turn it was to light the kerosene lamp, Dottie said she would tell us a ghost story. I don't remember where Mother and Louise had gone, but my sisters and I huddled together around a lamp on the table in the dark kitchen.

"One stormy night," she began, her voice low, her eyes wide. "This young guy, he was driving home on a dark, windy road. The rain was coming down hard, and thunder and lightning filled up the sky."

"Was he scared?" Gretchen asked, grabbing my hand.

"Well, wouldn't you be?" Dottie said. Everyone drew nearer as Dottie leaned forward in anticipation of the story she wanted to tell. "All of a sudden in a big flash of lightning he seen something ahead—a girl walking alongside the road wearing a long white dress."

"Was she all wet from the rain?" Gretchen asked, bouncing into my lap.

"Shut up. Let Dots tell us the story."

"He stopped the car and told her to get in ..." Dottie told her story masterfully as darkness pressed against my back like a big icy hand.

"So this guy, he asks her where she lives so he can drive her home. He can see that she's shivering with cold and takes off his jacket and tells her to put it around her shoulders."

Dottie paused and we all exchanged wary looks.

"When he got to her house, he could barely see it. It was so dark. But, there was one candle burning in the front window. Before he could say a word or go around to open the door for her—'cause this guy's a gentleman—the girl in the white dress opens the car door and runs. To tell you the truth, he would swear later that she vanished into thin air."

"I'm scared," Gretchen whispered in my ear. I cuddled her closer.

"So the next day the guy decided he would drive out to that old house to see if he could get his jacket back. When he got there it had already turned dark. He knocked and after a while this old lady opened the door. She looked old as the hills, all wrinkled, and had a wart on her nose just like a witch. He told her about seeing the girl in white on the road, giving her a ride and his jacket. Then he asked if he could have it back.

"The old lady shivered and said, 'When did you pick her up?' He told her it was last night. Now here is the story she told him. 'Last night was the thirtieth anniversary of my daughter's death. On a rainy night when she was only sixteen, she was killed on that road.'"

"The girl was a ghost!" Susan cried.

"I'm not finished yet." Dottie cleared her throat and carried on. "So, next thing the old woman said—because he'd looked at her like she was crazy—was, 'Come with me.' He followed her out behind the house to a bunch of old trees and one lonesome grave stone. It was her daughter's grave and there it was—his jacket hanging there, just like that girl knew he'd be coming for it."

Susan gasped, "Is that a true story?"

"Of course, it's true. My granny knew that old lady. She told me that story herself. She ain't never told a lie in her whole life," Dottie swore.

"That was *really* scary," I said, taking in the astonishment on my sisters' faces. "Now, I'll tell one I heard. It's called 'The Hand.'"

"I heard that one already," Dottie, said. "It's really swell. Tell it again."

Using my most spooky voice and the sound effects that come as a bloody hand taps its way across the kitchen table, I told the story.

*   *   *

The Catholic chapel, open every day for prayer, was one of our favorite haunts in Redstone. Ruth, the middle-aged lady who ran the only gift shop in the village, tended the chapel. A one-lady altar guild, she made everything ready for Sunday when a priest would come to say Mass. A couple of times during Dottie's stay we went to the chapel to watch Ruth dust and fuss around the altar, or count out the hosts and ready the vestments. We asked her questions like why she laid a little linen towel in a silver dish, and why she put water in one cruet and wine in another. We wanted to know about all the icons, who they were, and their stories. After we had turned Ruth's simple duties into a long morning's work, we ran off to gather wildflowers for the altar. Ruth appreciated that.

Dottie went to a Pentecostal Church where they talked against Catholics. She said she would have to keep her visits to the chapel a secret from her parents. But she thought Ruth was really nice and maybe, because of her, she wouldn't think that all Catholics were bad anymore. She liked all the pretty statues even though they were idols. Since she herself didn't pray to them she figured it wasn't a sin to admire them. I was glad my mother didn't care if we visited Ruth and had never once mentioned sin.

*   *   *

After Dottie went home, Mother and Louise took us to the Friday night barn dance. Folks came from Carbondale and all the little towns hidden in the mountains. A barn served as a dance hall with hay bales scattered around for seating and a refreshment table with all kinds of home baked-cookies, fudge, and strawberry Kool-Aid. Most of the local men brought their own refreshments, flasks of whiskey tucked into their jean's back pockets. The square dance caller had the microphone turned up high, his nasal voice overwhelming the fiddle, accordion, and guitar. Men stomping across the floor in cowboy boots and hats and women swinging around in a flurry of brightly ruffled skirts made the whole building shake.

Mother, Louise, my sisters, and I found partners and joined a square. We'd been square dancing before, so all we had to do was listen to the caller.

"Ladies to the center—and back to the bar—gents to the center and form a star—with a right hand cross and a howdy-do—and a left hand back and a how are you—pass your partner and take the next—gents swing out and ladies swing in—go full around and back again—break and swing and when you get right—everybody swing with all your might!"

I saw my mother's face light with fun as she twirled to the music, brushing shoulders with the cowboys and old men in our square. She looked like a young girl flushed and full of life, her skirt whirling, her ponytail bouncing around her face. I could hardly keep my eyes off her.

After the dance, on the drive home through the mountains, the stars whirling overhead, my mother teased Louise about the fiddle player. I guessed that he'd made a pass at her. Whatever passion burned between the cowboy and Louise had probably been fairly innocent because my mother teased her in front of us.

* * *

Full of wonders, the mountains gave us drifts of blue and white columbine, bright red Indian paintbrush, and hot springs pooling up in caves or percolating out of the rocks. On the road to Carbondale, someone had built a wooden shack around a hot spring where hot water, stinking of sulfur, trickled into a marble pool set into the hillside.

One day my mother parked the car on the edge of the road. We entered the shack and took off our clothes. I felt very grown-up sitting naked with Mother and Louise in my almost-a-woman body. I tried not to look at Louise's beautiful breasts, her full dark areolas bobbing at the surface of the water as she relaxed into the steam. I didn't like to see my mother naked because of her deeply scarred belly. The crisscross of painful-looking gashes had been cut so that my sisters and I could be born.

The women liked to soak for a long time in the hot, sulfur water. After they'd smoked one cigarette, I thought we'd had enough. But they were just getting started. They closed their eyes and relaxed against the marble seat carved into the side of the pool, talking lazily, soaking their cares away.

I was the outsider. They knew all about life—all the things I wanted to know. I didn't understand their laughter or the subtle looks that passed between them—something to do with the fiddle player. On another night, after the square dance, had Louise met him for drinks? I watched and listened, wondering what it would be like to be a woman and how long I would have to wait to find out.

8

Ferrari Girl

1952

"They [teenagers] are really like Ferraris with weak brakes." —Dr. Frances Jensen, The Teenage Brain

AFTER MY MOTHER painted the small room robin's egg blue with butter yellow trim, I moved into my own bedroom. A closet, bookshelves, and desk had been built at one end, leaving just enough space for a dresser and a twin bed. I loved my desk, a quiet place of my own where I could sit and write—a space to crawl out of my pretty-girl suit to become a girl who did not always agree with her friends, her mother, her church, or school. Writing carried me away to imaginary places or took me inside where I felt and believed. I didn't know how to go inside any other way. I had a philosophy of life and wrote down my heretical beliefs about Jesus, and how I knew that God was always with me, about the necessity of prayer, and how to find true happiness in life and in marriage. I really believed I knew the answers and needed to state them. I wanted to let the poor world know the answers to these problems. To read these little essays now is embarrassing and surprising.

I wrote a few short stories—one a romance I thought I'd send to *True Story* magazine. *The Awakening of Dream Boy* was about a girl who meets a shy boy and kisses *him* on the first date. *She* kissed him—that was the shocker and on a *first* date. You just didn't do that. *Boys* didn't even kiss girls on the first date. I even had a pen name: Mike Nerak (Karen spelled backwards) as a tribute to the writer George Eliot. Not that I'd read her books. Mother had told me about women in her time who did better if publishers thought they were men.

My scrapbook took up a good deal of time. I was much more devoted to it than to my studies as I carefully glued in souvenirs: matchbooks, menus, invitations, theatre tickets, a popcorn bag, letters, pictures I'd taken with my Brownie, and news clippings from the evening paper like a mushroom cloud over the New Mexico desert and Ethel and Julius Rosenberg in their coffins over a headline: "Atom Spies' Funeral Set for Today in New York."

We felt safer, knowing the Rosenbergs were dead. We thought a lot about the Communists. They were everywhere, determined to destroy our way of life. My mother was the only person I knew who scoffed at the Communist scare. She kept that to herself, but whenever the subject came up, I heard her grumble to herself about mass hysteria and fear. She was the only one in our family who voted for the Democrat, Senator Estes Kefauver, instead of General Dwight D. Eisenhower.

Having survived seventh and eighth grades, and eager to move up to high school, I could hardly wait to see what would happen to me next. My mother put the brakes on my lust for "too grown up for a freshman" adventures. She decided which movies I could see.

"My girlfriends get to see whatever they want," I whined.

She wouldn't allow me to date older boys who drove cars, or to go steady, or to go to sleepovers at homes she thought would not have the right adult supervision.

I appeared as a daily irritation to my mother in my carbon copy hairdo and fad-inspired clothes. And when I looked at her, I saw someone radically odd. I would have died rather than tell my girlfriends anything about her activities and tastes.

*   *   *

Peggy Ann kept a cedar hope chest at the foot of her bed. Most girls had hope chests: a place to collect and store things needed for eventual marriage. I had asked for one, but my mother thought they were silly, sentimental, old-fashioned. The chest had been used first by Peggy Ann's grandmother, passed on to her mother, and finally ended up with Peggy Ann.

She lifted the lid and let me look at all the small things on top: pillowcases she embroidered, doilies crocheted by her grandmother, an embroidered dresser scarf and damask tablecloth, and potholders and aprons that she had sewn. Enviously I watched Peggy tenderly unfold each treasure. Underneath a handmade quilt, sheets and blankets waited for the day she would make her marriage bed.

Deep down, when I really thought about it, I agreed with my mother. It seemed silly to dream over potholders. Yet as far as I could tell, that's what I'd be one day—a wife and mother. I didn't think about whether or not I wanted to marry. I just expected I would. No one had talked of college for me since the days before I started school when my mother and I had played library. (I was the librarian and she was the book borrower who returned her books late and had to pay me a penny fine.) The closest she ever got to mentioning my future was when she was mad at me and yelled, "I hope one day you'll have three children just like *you!*" People had stopped asking me what I wanted to be when I grew up. That seemed to be a question for little ones and for boys.

In my self-conscious, watchful, even fearful state, I was unable to think of anyone else but me. I could not enter a room full of people without pasting a smile on my face, tucking in my tummy, and lengthening my neck the way I'd learned while walking with a book on my head. My mother let me know every time I let my stomach relax or my shoulders slump or my chin sink or my face fall slack.

"Close your mouth, Karen. You look like the village idiot."

I could not walk down the street without looking at my reflection in store windows as I passed. I didn't look to admire myself, but to make sure I walked right or that my hair didn't need a comb, or that I hadn't suddenly turned into a goon.

My deepest desire had nothing to do with learning what they taught in school or making the grades that would please my father. I just wanted to be popular. Even though I had studied with interest the most adored older girls, I could not be sure what made them so well liked. Finally, I found the courage to ask the school's most popular senior girl if she would tell me her secret.

I stopped her on her way to her car in the high school parking lot.

"I have a question—I hope you'll tell me—I mean—what can I do to be as popular as you?"

Priscilla, the homecoming queen, didn't laugh in my face. She smiled sweetly. "It's simple really," she said without taking a moment to think. "Just be friendly. Smile at people and say hello. Be actually glad to see them."

"Really? What about my looks and clothes?"

"You are already pretty and have nice clothes—just be sincere with people—care about them and be friendly."

I went away with a plan. I would be the friendliest girl at Grand Junction High School.

* * *

Most of my classes bored me. History was a big yawn. Mr. Timms was so boring he fell asleep during his own lectures. I was hopeless in algebra. "I will never use this stuff," I announced, "just teach me to balance a checkbook!" I liked to sew, draw and paint, and write stories and poems. I wanted to write for the school newspaper, but they wouldn't let me because of the Cs in English. I couldn't get As and Bs because Miss Conway hated me. She made that plain when she called roll on the first day of class.

Peering at me over her glasses she sniffed, "I had both your mother and father when they were in high school. I certainly hope that you are a better student then they were!"

I wrote a short story for her class and after she read and graded it, and was handing the student's stories back, she held mine up in front of the class and said, "This is too well written. Karen, I don't think you wrote it."

When I told Mother about Miss Conway's insulting remark, she shrugged her shoulders and said, "That's what's called a back-handed compliment. Just ignore it."

To confuse me further, Miss Conway had given me a rare A–.

*   *   *

I first knew Mother was ill when our father pulled us aside one morning before school. He spoke softly, matter-of-factly, his eyes grave with concern. He said she would have to stay in bed and rest. He wanted us to keep noise to a minimum, to let her sleep all day if she wanted.

"What's the matter with her?"

"Oh, well, she had that toothache—you know. Having that wisdom tooth pulled seemed to take a lot out of her."

Cousin Jo took my little sister on weekends. Mrs. Ryan babysat, cooked, and cleaned. Though my father had explained about the wisdom tooth, worry plagued me. Not long before, out in California, Mother's brother Dick had dropped dead in his driveway from a massive heart attack. Following his death my mother changed. The effects of shock and sorrow made her withdraw. I had never seen her cry before. And when she got sick from her wisdom tooth and lay in bed day after day, I worried that the same thing could happen to her. I suspected that our father hadn't told us the truth. I believed that Mother had had a heart attack.

Concerned that she might be sleeping, I knocked very softly on the door to her room and listened for her "Come in." I opened the door and once inside the darkened room closed it gently. "How are you feeling, Mother?" I asked, crossing gingerly to her side of the bed.

"I'm okay," she said, trying to rouse herself. "Would you open the drapes for me?"

"Sure," I said, pulling the traverse cord. "Can I sit down?"

"Yes—please," she breathed, her dry lips stretching oddly into a misshapen smile.

I sat on the bed beside her and as I leaned in to hug her, she reached for my hand. She smelled musty and her hair looked oily and I started to cry.

"I'm all worried about you."

"Oh, Karen, please—" she said, her eyes pooling with tears. "I'm going to be just fine."

"What's the matter with you? Tell me the truth—is it your heart?"

"No, no, my heart's just fine. I promise. I'm going to feel much better in a little while. I just let myself get too tired and I had that awful tooth pulled."

"How long do you have to stay in bed?"

"Just a little longer," she said.

Feeling reassured, I got her a drink of water and left her to sleep. She had convinced me that she just needed rest and the dental surgery would heal. Mother lay in bed for some time longer. Long enough to keep me worried. Then one day she got dressed and went downtown. She bought herself a portable typewriter, set up a workspace in the bedroom, and began writing the stories she wanted to tell. After that she seemed better.

Many years later my cousin told me that Mother had had a nervous breakdown. She knew about it because it was her mother who had taken care of Gretchen during my mother's illness.

Life had been too hard for Bette, even from her sickly childhood perhaps. Knowing what I know now, I believe she felt she had to bear up under everything all alone, to be brave, self-reliant, untouched by human weakness or tragedy. She struggled with her anger, truly thinking it arose from some force she could squelch intellectually. She seemed to think that normal emotions like disappointment, sadness, and grief were nothing more than self-pity. From her sister and her friends, I learned that she never talked about her struggles. I think her struggle to become who she was born to be was more than she could bear. Like the morning glories blooming along the arid roadside on the outskirts of town, she had tried to bloom in the desert that was her life.

A deadly silence raged inside our parent's marriage. Except when they discussed the mechanics of the day, my mother and father had nothing to say to one another.

"Do you and Daddy still love each other?" I asked. "You don't hug and kiss anymore." I remembered the days when my father kissed her every day, wrapping her in both of his arms, spinning her off her feet. How happy they had looked. Even though I had watched from across the room, I felt part of their embrace.

She seemed startled by my question. Considering her answer, she turned away and opened the refrigerator door. "When you've been married a long time," she said softly to the refrigerator, "you don't act the way you used to." She took a covered dish from the shelf and placed it on the kitchen counter. A personal question had been asked and she had finally recovered. "After a while you don't have to say so much about love to one another."

My mother moved out of the master bedroom. She slept in the living room on the thinking bench. Mornings we found her still asleep, cuddled up with her current book, her body entwined with a blanket.

*   *   *

The last days of my freshman year, after spring's warm air had come to a boil and I thought school would never end, our family went to my sister Susan's Girl Scout picnic in Hawthorne Park. Leaning against the trunk of a tree, I sat down to eat. Halfway through my chiliburger I got the feeling that someone was watching me. I looked up to see Steve Hartsfield sitting across the lawn at a picnic table with his family. He was the son of a prominent lawyer, the kind of boy my father could proudly mention to his fellow Kiwanians.

He'd stopped eating and was staring at me. We both dropped our eyes to our paper plates. When he got up and walked toward me, I caught my breath and risked a smile.

"How about coming for a ride around the park a few times?" he said, skipping the usual boy gestures—shuffling, shoe staring, and trying to look like it didn't matter if I said yes or no.

"I'll ask my mother." I hoped my heart and my mind would stop flying around. Shirley had told me that Steve was a wolf. But she thought that about all the boys so I didn't know if I should believe her. I walked across the lawn where my mother chatted with a friend. In case Steve was watching I held in my tummy and put just the right amount of sway into my hips—not enough to be obvious—but just the right swing to look really sophisticated. My mother knew Steve's parents and said it would be okay. For the moment, she must have forgotten her rules about older boys with cars.

Steve drove a shiny dark green Ford convertible. Like a gentleman he opened the car door, and I climbed in. Dumbstruck, I sank into the soft leather upholstery.

"Let's drag Main," he said, driving off into the hot desert air, the breeze suddenly cooling.

On Main Street, we passed other kids in their cars—many of them friends. He honked and we waved. As we drove past neon signs flashing Fashion Bar, Out West Bootery, and Mesa Drug, I loved being seen with Steve.

I liked him. His blue eyes looked open and friendly. He didn't act like a wolf even though he was very handsome and tall and could get any girl he wanted. We talked about the kids we knew in common and our classes at school.

"Does your mother let you go out much?" he asked on our way back to the park.

"She lets me go on dates, if that's what you mean."

"Do you think you could go to a show tomorrow night? 'Cause I'm leaving Saturday morning for Wyoming."

"Wyoming?"

"Yeah, I'm going to work on a ranch over there and I'd like to take you out before I leave." He smiled at me openly, like one adult addressing another adult.

"I'll talk it over with my mother and tell you tomorrow." That was all right with Steve, and we hurried back to the park.

Later that night, when I told my mother about it, she looked worried. "Your Daddy and I made a rule that you're not allowed to date upperclassmen. I'd like to let you go but . . ."

"Oh, Mother, pleeeze," I begged.

"Well—he has awfully nice parents."

"Thanks, Mother." I kissed her multiple times on the cheek and vanished before she could change her mind.

I don't remember anything about our first date except that we went to the movies. But Steve left for Wyoming and I went back to church camp in the mountains. I dated lots of different boys all summer long. "Safety in numbers!" my mother said.

*   *   *

Meeting Steve so impressed me that I decided to write about it. My fascinating life, I thought, provided me with loads of material for a book. I would write about the joys and pains of teenage life. Maybe that would be the title: *The Joy and Pain of Teenage Life by a Real Teenager*. My book would begin with the story of how I met Steve and from that pinnacle flash back to my happy carefree childhood in a small town in the West. The book would reveal how I had remade myself, a hopelessly awkward tomboy who lived in trees and on the backs of wild Indian ponies, into the lovely creature that Steve would want to date. Other girls could learn from my experience. I had lots of good advice. I wrote exactly five and one-third narrow-lined notebook pages before I got writer's cramp and quit.

*   *   *

For generations of summers, Lincoln Park had been a favorite destination for high school kids. The park ran the length of four blocks under stately old trees shading an emerald lawn bordering the tennis courts and ball field.

Before the baseball game our gang of girlfriends stopped at The Smoke Shack across the street from the park. Dressed exactly alike in jeans and swallowed up by our father's white dress shirts, we squeezed into the largest booth. Our hair styles and makeup were identical—shoulder-length curls with Mamie Eisenhower bangs and bright red lipstick. We ordered cheeseburgers, fries, and cherry cokes. Soon the place filled up with folks hoping to eat before the

game. Among the crowd were the gang of boys my friends and I had
hung out with since seventh grade.

In plenty of time before the game, we left the restaurant, crossed the
street, and entered the park. The boys followed close behind, horsing
around under the trees with the girls on the dark expanse of lawn.

I was afraid of the boys—not because of the dark or the
expectant flurry of excitement in the air—I was leery of them in
broad daylight. Even though I'd been around them since seventh
grade, I didn't really know them as friends. Back on Teller Avenue
when I was small, boys tied me to a tree and ran away, and big boys
on bikes chased me down Sixth Street. Mother frequently
admonished me to stay away from "those boys." And Daddy said
that boys didn't like girls who beat them at games. Further, he'd said
I shouldn't get upset when boys teased because "that means they
like you." On top of that, there was the old man next door. When I
was little he took me on his lap to read me the funny papers and put
his finger inside my panties. Recently, when I was alone walking
back to school from the park after lunch, a man parked his car up
ahead and opened the passenger car door. He called to me as I
passed and when I looked at him he smiled, holding his big white
thing, stroking it. He scared me so much I lost one of my shoes
running and had to go back and pick it up.

When I told Mother that I was afraid of boys she said that not
having brothers had affected me adversely. My boy cousins lived far
away, and my too-busy father had no time to give me the "male
point of view." Mother left me with the impression that there was
something mysterious about boys that only fathers, brothers, and
male cousins could illuminate.

In the park with all these boys, I remembered our history together.
Like the night Hal kissed me. After a party, he'd jerked me into the
bushes. His passionate, wetly thrilling kiss had surprised me. In all the
years I'd known him, we had never said more than hello.

There in Lincoln Park, the boys yelled for the girls to wait up,
spreading out among us as we all headed toward the splash of bright
light surrounding the distant ballfield. After we walked a while I
noticed that my girlfriends had banded together and moved ahead. I
picked up my pace. I didn't like being the only girl loping along with

the boys, even though they joked among themselves and didn't seem to notice me.

The moment I picked up speed, they did too. My girlfriends had disappeared into the expanse of darkness falling between them and the ballpark. I decided to make a run for it.

I could hear seven boys sprinting close behind, the pounding of their feet on the lawn, their lungs pumping air. Something had changed. All of a sudden, I was running through an electrical field charged with danger. Someone grabbed me by the arm and threw me down. I yelped with surprise as my breath left my body. Hands grabbed and pressed me against the lawn. Black silhouettes rose over me, almost faceless against the starry sky.

"Stop! No! No!"

Two of them sounded out of breath as they pinned down my arms. One was on top of me. I could not move and was crying. He tried to kiss me, but I flung my head from side to side and screamed.

"Let me go! Let me go!"

Out of the dark, a hand came hard over my mouth to muffle my cries. Other hands pinned my arms and legs to the lawn. I could barely breathe from the weight of so many. They growled, scuffled, and swore at one another like dogs fighting over a bone. My jeans were unbuttoned. I tried to kick at them.

A deep, commanding, voice sounded from somewhere above. "That's enough."

The lone figure grabbed hold of Bobby's arm and pulled him off. It was Frankie, the shy boy I barely knew. He had not laid a hand on me.

"Leave her alone!" he said, and Tony got to his feet. Nick followed.

Frankie reached out to me. I gratefully took his hand and let him help me up. I was too afraid to thank him or to blast the others with words of contempt. I ran as fast as I could toward the ballpark. Still feeling the terror of being chased by the boys, I was too frightened to look over my shoulder to see that they hadn't followed. No, I worried about how I looked. The girls would wonder about my smeared lipstick and messy hair. Feeling guilty, I tried to smooth my father's shirt and frantically searched my pockets for my lipstick and comb.

*   *   *

In bed before sleep, I tried putting the boys and what had happened out of my mind. A heaviness lay over me and I could not catch my breath. As an asthmatic, I had learned to sit up straight, prop my pillow against the headboard, and lean back to ease my breathing. It terrified me to lie down in the dark in my own bed like I was forced lie on the lawn. I got up, opened the door a crack to let in the hall light, and climbed back into bed, resting my back against the pillow again. I pulled up the covers and looked out the window at the cottonwood leaves turning in the breeze, catching the moonlight.

Do the boys think I'm a bad girl? I didn't ask Mother. I was afraid to tell her what happened.

Karen and Bette, 1940

Karen, posing as a "nice girl" in her senior portrait, 1956

Jim at Ventura Junior College, 1958

Karen in Fashion, Catalina Players, 1957

Karen and Susan (background) with Lucky, 1942

Karen in her new ducktail haircut and homemade formal gown, 1955

Bette in her studio

Karen in *The Prince of Liars*,
Catalina Players, 1957

9

Sexy

1953

"I am good, but not an angel. I do sin, but I am not the devil. I am just a small girl in a big world trying to find someone to love." —Marilyn Monroe

WHEN STEVE CAME home from Wyoming, he took me out to dinner and over dessert asked me to be his girl. I gratefully accepted, knowing I would begin my sophomore year confidently. My boyfriend was a handsome upperclassman, a popular baseball player, from a good family.

Steve took me to see *Niagara*, Marilyn Monroe's first starring role in a film. I had never seen her before, and there she was bigger than life up there on the screen, sex personified. I was shocked and bewildered by the blonde's wiggly walk, her tiny breathy voice, her lips twitching as if each word deserved a kiss. She was filmed in bed wearing nothing but a clinging white sheet as she and her lover dreamed up ways for him to murder her husband played by Joseph Cotton. I loved Joseph Cotton.

A few years ago, I watched *Niagara* again and was surprised by my memories of it. Now desensitized, I wondered what had been wrong with me as I sat beside Steve in the dark intensely embarrassed. During a passionate scene between Marilyn and her lover, Steve squeezed my hand. I yanked it away. I didn't want him to think that I approved of the animal attraction on display or guess that I had secret desires good girls never had.

After the show, without a word, we drove off toward my home in the country. Steve was in a spell of some sort and I was deeply disturbed. After a while I felt uncomfortable with the silence and had to say something.

"That was just terrible! She can't act. I think she's disgusting and silly."

"She's not that bad," Steve said, rolling his eyes as if Marilyn had already become a delicious private memory.

"Well, she certainly can't act—you can't say she can act!"

"She acted well enough to convince you."

"I don't want to talk about it."

I crossed my arms and shriveled against the passenger door, blaming Marilyn for—I didn't know what. Someone had to take the blame for all the crossed messages. Have sex and ruin your reputation. Have sex and ecstasy will be yours. I'd already tasted a bite of the ecstasy that came with Steve's kisses.

When Steve pulled into the driveway, I pecked him on the cheek. "Goodnight. I'll walk myself to the door."

He smiled at me like he thought I was very young.

* * *

Soon Steve gave me his class ring. We were going steady, and Mother did not protest. After the Sadie Hawkins Day dance where we were voted King and Queen of the dance, he parked in our driveway. We talked and necked—kissing, accompanied by a little heavy breathing. Steve was a gentleman. He wanted to become a lawyer like his father. Knowing what he wanted and how to achieve it, he talked about going away to college in the fall. He sounded smart enough to make everything work just exactly the way it should. He would follow the rules, achieve his dreams, and have a wonderful life.

Under a sky full of stars, Nat King Cole was singing on the car radio. Steve talked about his car and a coming football game. I wasn't listening intently, just entranced by the song. He stopped talking and listened a moment, then interrupted my feelings with more words.

"Did you know he's a Negro?"

Steve said he could prove it. He had a magazine at home with pictures. I'd seen Negroes in movies like *Gone with the Wind* and *Show Boat* but never one in person and as far I knew none lived in Grand Junction.

The following year I became aware of two students who were black. One was a shy girl and the other a bold athlete—a football star. He was so popular that we elected him student body president. It's astonishing now to look at the high school annual from 1955 and see him in juxtaposition to our school mascot the tiger, the cartoon figure of Little Black Sambo in a football uniform, filling in all the empty spaces.

All I wanted was for Steve to stop talking, to kiss and hold me. Except for that one unbelievable comment about my favorite singer, I didn't find his conversation interesting. I wondered if he was going to turn into one of those ordinary men Mother had warned me about. As I understood it, I should look for an intellectual or one studying to be one. He should love great books, art, and music—especially books. Steve loved his car, baseball, and Marilyn Monroe.

I leaned back against the seat and gazed up at the stars. Steve's voice droned on, and I threw both arms in back of my head, cradled my neck in my hands, sighed, and closed my eyes.

Steve stopped talking. "Come here, Baby," he said, pulling me into his arms. He kissed me for a long time, and when my desire had built to unacceptable levels, he pulled away and looked at my face in the moonlight.

"It's time you go inside."

"I don't want to." I burrowed into his arms. I wanted to hear him say he loved me. He kissed me lightly, pulled away, got out of the car, and walked around to open the passenger door. Taking me by the hand, he led me to the front door.

"Goodnight, Baby," he sighed. "I'll call you tomorrow."

Steve was boring. I wanted him to be in love with me.

* * *

The week after I broke up with Steve, Lenny asked me to the Friday night dance at the high school gym. I'd danced with him before and thought he was the best dancer in school. Lenny had an appealing aura of adventure about him.

In Grand Junction, high school dances relied on two big speakers playing pop tunes and big band swing music from the forties. Rock and roll hadn't been invented, and rhythm and blues hadn't been heard in those mountains. I loved to swing dance. We called it the boogie. With Lenny in the lead I was in my element. Together we tore up the floor to Benny Goodman's "In the Mood." Then Artie Shaw sweetened the air with his clarinet and "Moonglow." I melted in Lenny's strong arms as his confident footwork carried us off on a dream, and when the drum brushed us apart, we swung to the beat. He fastened his eyes on me, and every time I felt shy and looked away, he tugged at my hand and wouldn't let me hide.

After the dance, he drove out to the country and parked his car on a lonely canal road beside a thick grove of trees. He switched off the ignition and turned to look at me.

Before I could say a word, he pounced, kissing me hotly.

Even though you weren't supposed to kiss on your first date, I wanted to kiss him. But first I'd hoped we would talk and hold hands. Maybe he would say sweet things to me like he'd always wanted to date me. Then our first date would end with a dreamy goodnight kiss.

Lenny was scaring me. "I barely know you," I said trying to be as nice as I could as I pushed him away.

"Look, Baby, you dance like you want to get laid."

"I do not!" I disagreed wholeheartedly.

"What's all that hot stuff then? You are the hottest boogie babe I've ever seen."

"I am not! It's just feeling the music—it's dancing. It doesn't mean that."

"What else could it mean," he said, grabbing me for another kiss.

"Lenny, no." I was whining as my head plunged into terrible confusion.

"I know what you want better than you do," he said, letting his arms fall. He turned on the ignition and raced the engine. His muffler roared.

"There's a name for girls like you—cock tease."

He backed down the road at full speed. Terrified, I held on to the hand rest as he spun onto the paved road and raced toward my house. When he pulled into the driveway, I got out, slammed the door, and ran up the front walk. I would never speak to the dreamboat again.

* * *

I had made a terrible mistake. Steve deserved a second chance. Luckily he didn't hold a grudge and invited me to the homecoming dance. Not long after, he asked me to the movies. *Gentlemen Prefer Blondes* starring Marilyn Monroe was playing.

Recently Marilyn had appeared nude in the first *Playboy*. The boys were saying, "I wouldn't kick *her* out of bed!"

"I really don't like Marilyn Monroe very much," I said.

"It's not like *Niagara*," Steve promised. "It's a musical comedy."

Dripping with red sequins and confidence, Marilyn sang "Diamonds Are a Girl's Best Friend." She played it sweet, dumb, and funny, as she and her friends plotted to marry wealthy men. I enjoyed the show. Afterwards, sitting outside in his car, Steve closed his eyes and spoke dreamily of Marilyn—teasing about her platinum blonde hair, milky white skin, and fire engine red lipstick.

"She is *so* sexy."

The first time someone said that I was sexy, I asked Mother what it meant.

"It means you are appealing to the opposite sex."

By that definition, I thought, it is okay to be sexy. But if Marilyn was sexy, that gave new meaning to the word. She deliberately tried to arouse men. That meant that I had to ask myself a question. *Do I want to arouse the boys?* Lenny thought so—he accused me of that.

After the movie when Steve kissed me I could feel his heart beating fast. His hand came out of the dark and lingered at my waist. Then so tenderly, he touched my breast. I wanted him to touch me. I didn't say no. I believed that all those feelings were happening because he finally loved me.

Steve stopped himself. He sighed and said, "You're trouble." Immediately he got out of the car and walked me to the door. I sensed that I should not try to cajole him or protest.

He never asked me out again.

*   *   *

I had seen the red convertible pull in and out of the school parking lot, but I had never spoken to the driver. When Reggie stopped me on the lawn at the high school, he asked how I liked one of my classes. He seemed shy and mentioned being friends with Steve.

"Steve says it's okay if I ask you out."

Shuddering inside, I hoped and prayed I wasn't blushing or that Steve didn't tell him what I let him do. Reggie asked me to the Demolay dinner dance.

I wasn't allowed to buy a new gown for the dance and didn't have time to make one. I had to wear the same gown I'd worn to the Christmas formal with Steve. The same strapless baby blue formal with the dyed to match shoes. Reggie brought a corsage of pink rosebuds, and I pinned it to my waist. As we drove off in his convertible I heaved a sigh, put on a scarf, and took a look at my date. He was very good-looking in his dark suit—dark hair and eyes, big and well built, just like a quarterback should be. He smelled of after shave. I'd never dated a football star before.

Our first dance it was plain to see Reggie was too tall, leaving me eye-to-eye with his lapel. As he led me around the hotel ballroom, he didn't seem to hear the music and aimlessly used an all-purpose box waltz. I missed Steve as a dance partner.

By the end of a month-long whirlwind of dates with Reggie to the show, dinners out at the best restaurants, and parties with friends, we were going steady. I loved being his girl. The night of the Sweetheart Formal I wore a new pink evening gown. Reggie gave me an orchid corsage and Valentine chocolates in a red heart-shaped box. Both made it into my scrapbook: the corsage, dried up after fifty years, and the flattened candy box with its red velvet ribbon were finally discarded in about 2004.

At the dance, I was elected sophomore attendant to the senior queen. The class president escorted me to the stage to join the queen's court. Looking out over the crowd of kids watching the ceremony, I saw Reggie and could tell he was proud. Following the ceremony, it was his turn to come onstage and lead me back to the dance floor.

All that excitement and splendor—proof that I was popular— didn't make my head swim half as much as what I learned in the ladies' room. One of my girlfriends said that the Sweetheart Queen— senior Alice Thatcher—had had sex with her boyfriend. The source of the news was irrefutable: Alice's little brother had caught them.

* * *

Reggie said he loved me and I believed him. I felt loved for the first time in my life. I cherished his kisses and how it felt when he touched me. I couldn't help myself. I loved his smile, the twinkle in his eyes, his fascination with me, the way he teased, his eagerness to be alone with me every day. In his arms I was adored.

After church one Sunday Reggie drove me home with one arm while the other pressed me close. I cuddled near, kissing his throat as I undid his tie. He pulled into a wooded spot off the road, turned off the ignition, unbuttoned his shirt and pulled my dress down to the waist. Bare skin against bare skin, we kissed until our lips were sore. We decided to make love the next time we met—he would be prepared.

Mother decided it was time for me to learn the facts of life. Not knowing how to tell me herself, she made an appointment with Dr. Graves. Welcoming us into his examination room, he patted the examination table and I hopped up, highly uncomfortable with two adults staring at me—the girl who needs to know a thing or two about men.

Mother explained that she had suddenly realized that I was growing up. It might be time, she thought, for Dr. Graves to explain some things about young men— "what they are like, you know."

Listening, Dr. Graves held his chin in one hand and looked at the floor. When she had finished describing the reason we were there, the room fell silent. He began to pace. I could tell he was thinking. Shortly he arrived at the foot of the examination table, face to face with me.

"You see, Karen," he said loosening his tie with one finger, "inside your body is a little house where babies will come to live one day."

"I know," I said, mortified.

Reassuring me, he took both of my hands before he said another word. "What happens is this. The little house fills up with groceries every month and if no child comes to live there, then all the groceries fall out and that is your period." He looked suddenly lost for words.

"I know," I said, remembering all the times he held my hand when I was small and sick. I felt nothing but love and gratitude for all he'd done and ashamed that Mother was torturing him.

He looked away then let my hands fall, stepping back a bit. He turned toward the window with his back to me.

"When it comes to young men, Karen, the best thing I can tell you is don't ever get into the back seat of a car with a boy."

That was it. I had received formal sex education—too late.

Not a word was spoken between us as Mother and I drove home. The atmosphere burned with the tension and silence of fast-held secrets. Neither of us knew how to break through it.

*   *   *

Why was I so different from my mother's generation when it came to sex? Was it the songs on the radio or *Playboy* or Marilyn? Was it Dr. Spock or Dr. Kinsey and his books on human sexuality? Was it a hangover from World War II when men and women were thrown together into a new world of work and sex? Or the movies where we saw bad girls in action?

When married film star Ingrid Bergman fell in love with Italian director Roberto Rossellini in 1949, divorce was uncommon. She became pregnant with Rossellini's son, causing a huge scandal in the United States, where she was denounced from the floor of the Senate by Edwin C. Johnson, our senator from Colorado. He said she was "a horrible example of womanhood and a powerful influence for evil." There was a floor vote, and Bergman was banned from making films in the United States. The scandal forced her to flee to Italy, where she gave birth to twin daughters by Rossellini. Her husband, Dr. Petter Lindström, eventually sued for desertion and waged a custody battle. We followed every word of the scandal in the newspapers, and no one I knew spoke up for Bergman.

The fifties were different from the sexual revolution of the sixties and seventies. When we made love in cars we believed we were bad. We were not exercising our right to be just like the boys. We were involved in something that could ruin our lives and shame our families. If your daughter or big sister got "knocked up" you had two choices: leave town and give the baby up for adoption or get married and hope that no one counted the months between the wedding day and the birth of your child. Still we would sacrifice everything for the overpowering desire for love in secret places. We believed it was love—the concept of *lust* was foreign. Yes, it was love, irresistible, uncontrollable love and the first time I felt truly loved was with Reggie.

*   *   *

By early summer Reggie had changed. He wasn't sweet to me any longer. We fought all the time, mostly because he didn't want me to have any kind of life apart from him. He hated it when I wanted to go riding with Peggie Ann on weekends. He seemed jealous if I went to a friend's birthday party on a Saturday night. He no longer spent any time with his friends. I was his whole life. Soon, I withdrew from everything but Reggie.

That spring I was asked to pose for a photograph for *The Uranium Digest*, a local trade magazine. They wanted to announce Miss Atomic Energy contest and needed a pretty girl in a swimsuit to pose wearing the crown. Too young to be a contestant, I agreed to put on my white one-piece swimsuit and wear a metal crown with the symbol of the atom at its apex. The black and white picture ran in the May issue. It appeared about the time of my seventeenth birthday, when my mother and father announced their plans to divorce and I found out I was pregnant.

10

Secrets

1955

I SAW MY mother cry twice, once when her brother died and again on the day I came home from school for lunch and found her waiting for me in the kitchen. Before she spoke, before the tears, I noticed how ill she looked. She was terribly thin, her skin tinged gray, the blue sky of her eyes clouded. For a long time, I'd been too absorbed in myself and Reggie to notice my mother.

For weeks Reggie and I had worried that I was pregnant. But he knew what to do. He told me to pee in a little bottle and asked a married friend to take it to his wife's doctor. After a few torturous days, we heard that I was pregnant.

I thought the world had come to an end, but Reggie seemed strong. Suddenly thoughtful and concerned, he said he wanted to marry me. Neither of us breathed a word to anyone.

At night, thinking about what was growing inside me, I couldn't sleep. I lay awake looking out the window through cottonwood leaves to the moon, whispering a prayer. "O, God, help me. Make it not happen. Make it go away." I'd heard about using a coat hanger, but I didn't know how.

Lying in bed I promised God, "If you make me not pregnant, I'll never be bad again." I held my breath for a long time, dissolving into the sheets, trying to make my heart stop. If I want to, I thought, I can will myself to die. Lying there, asking the life to drift out of my body, dizzy from the desire to be no more, I thought, *The last thing I'll see is the unfeeling moon.*

Mother had not made lunch. I wondered why she looked so strange. I don't remember anything she said before: "Your father and I are getting a divorce."

She burst into tears and opened her arms for me. "If I go on living with him I'll die," she sobbed.

I moved into her embrace, blinked back a frenzy of confusion and tears, and for her sake, put a stop on my emotions. As everything outside her pain vanished, I tried to comfort her. I didn't ask why. I knew why. Somehow, I'd always known that the marriage was wrong, but I'd never let myself *think* it.

"I don't know how to tell your sisters—they're so young. I'll break their hearts," she sobbed. "Especially Gretchen," she moaned, as if the thought caused her physical pain. Then she dropped a second bombshell.

"We are moving to California."

California?

"Gretchen is so fond of your father. I don't know what they'll do without each other." She shook her head solemnly and said, "You have to promise me that you won't tell anyone. Not Reggie. Not anyone—at least for a while. I'll let you know when you can tell your friends—but not a word to your grandmother. Promise me!"

Knowing I'd been entrusted with a terrible secret, I drove back to school in tears and spent the afternoon in a fog. In study hall, I looked at the kids—some of whom I'd known all my life. *I'll never see them again. I'll just disappear.* I wondered if my grandfather had sat at the very same desk. And if the faded two-tone paint job on the study hall walls had been the same when my parents sat here. The dark oak moldings and the floors seemed suddenly dear to me. *I'll be a stranger my senior year.*

Maybe it's for the best. I wouldn't have to marry Reggie. Maybe I could give the baby up for adoption and make a new life for myself. I folded my arms on the wooden desk and buried my head. Keeping our horrible secrets, I breathed in the fragrance of the old wood and dropped tears on a carved heart pierced by an arrow.

I wore our secrets like a coat of shame. Remembering my mother's mysterious illness and the weeks she'd stayed in bed, I was scared that she would die. Terrified that the strain of telling my sisters might kill her, I hurried home after school, walked to the end of our lane, and waited for Susan's bus.

Falling into step beside my sister, we made small talk as we walked up the road, past the cherry tree loaded with hard green fruit. Everything looked different to me—the rutted road, flies buzzing around ripening mulberries on the Helgerson's tree, their dingy house crying for a coat of paint.

Just as we passed the Helgerson's kitchen door, I said, "Whatever happens today, promise me you won't cry."

She turned to look at me. Her eyes hit me like a bullet. "Mother and Daddy are getting a divorce," she said as if she had known all along.

I shouldn't have worried about Susan. She had always intuited people and circumstances better than I. While I was at the center of a storm, Susan knew how to step back from the scene and melt into the walls where she could protect her back and see what was going on around her. She knew a lot about the people she lived with.

Mother must have suggested that Daddy talk to us about the divorce. I can't imagine that it was his idea to invite his daughters to dinner. We drove in silence to the restaurant he had selected, the Top Hat Drive-in, where we could sit in the car away from other people, where he wouldn't have to look at us around a table. Instead, from the driver's seat, he could stare at the neon top hat flashing brightly overhead and we could look at the back (or in my case from the passenger seat, the side) of his head. Our eyes would never have to meet. Slowly we choked down cheeseburgers as he explained that neither he nor our mother disliked one another, neither of them were bad people, but they had grown apart and would be happier living separate lives. He was sorry that this would disrupt our lives.

Gretchen wept openly as both Susan and I wiped tears off our cheeks, but we anxiously reassured him that we wanted happy parents. We all agreed that their happiness was the most important thing.

* * *

On the last day of May, after the last day of school, we packed our summer clothes. The rest of our clothes, my mother's half of the furniture, and her cash divorce settlement would come later, after we were settled in California. On the first night of June our father drove us to the airport, where Reggie waited for us outside the terminal. He got out of his car as we approached, nervously running his fingers through his crew-cut. He'd never been comfortable around my family. It seemed odd to me that he was there at all; we'd said goodbye to each other the night before.

My family moved through the terminal like a funeral procession with Reggie and me in the rear. My father had no idea of the trouble we were in. But after that night when she'd come into my bedroom to ask if my period had started, I'd told Reggie that my mother knew.

Though they tried to be brave, my sisters sobbed and clung to our father. I hugged Reggie's arm and tried to shake off the feeling that in some way I'd said goodbye to my father long ago. Our mother stood quietly apart, grief etched into her face, watching us. I couldn't bear to let all that sadness inside me. Then, just before we turned and walked toward the plane, I saw Mother reach out to touch Daddy's hand. Their eyes met for a painful second. She turned away and I saw his mouth move, "Goodbye."

An unnaturally chilly wind blew across the tarmac. I shivered as I climbed the steps and looked over my shoulder at Daddy and Reggie below. Both looked small and desolate, their heads tipped up, watching me wave goodbye. Now, looking back, I see them both clearly. They were much alike—isolated and lonely.

The plane taxied out on the runway gathering speed. I could feel the mighty thrust of the engines behind us, like a great omniscient hand lifting us out of the valley where we were born. For as long as I could, I watched a lone car heading west on the highway, wondering if it was Reggie. It seemed wicked that in that sad darkness, my heart beat with excitement. I looked out at the stars, bright as the lights of the town, happy that I was flying away. In seconds, Grand Junction disappeared from my window and I cried tears of relief.

11

Shangri-la

Ojai
1955

Shangri-la: A remote beautiful imaginary place where life approached perfection. —Merriam Webster Dictionary

SOON AFTER WE settled in the house on Shady Lane, Mother drove her brand new 1955 Chevrolet—aqua blue—fifteen miles through the hills to the coast. She walked a quarter mile out on the Ventura pier and looked over the ocean, green blue with little whitecaps from the wind. Water swelled below and beside her as far as she could see. To ground herself, she may have turned and looked back over the town to the waterfront buildings, the scores of green palms, and the blue-brown mountains where Ojai nested. At the very top of one of the hills there were two identical trees like sentries keeping watch over the city.

Raising her left hand for a look at her wedding and engagement rings, she let the diamonds sparkle in the sun and must have thought back to the time when she had loved him. Then, unable to remember why, she tugged the rings off her finger and dropped them one by one into the water. She watched them fall and disappear, willing the last flashes of sparkle to heal her.

* * *

In Ojai, Mother seemed transformed. The first thing I noticed was that she cleaned the house and even cooked with some interest. Saying nothing about my amazement, I watched her cut a recipe for borscht out of the newspaper. In Ojai, her tension and anger had all but disappeared. Away from Grand Junction and her husband, she seemed focused, even happy, and no longer succumbed to her rages.

Sitting together outside under the vine-covered arbor in our new butterfly chairs, I wanted to talk about it. "You seem happy, Mother. Are you happy now?"

"There's no such thing as happiness." Her eyes were fixed on something—or nothing—across the garden.

Those were fighting words. "Of course there is. How can you say that?"

"'Man is the artificer of his own happiness.' Thoreau said that— and he's right." She gave me her lofty look. "We have to make our happiness. Happiness doesn't just hover above, ready to drop in on us." She sounded sarcastic.

"I just wanted to know if you feel happy now—after the divorce—here in Ojai."

"I read about this yesterday." She looked frustrated in her search for the right words. "Emerson said it. Just a minute, I'll get the book."

She wasn't going to answer my question. As she dashed into the house to retrieve the book, I prepared myself for the offensive to come. My mother was about to relieve her pent-up need for intellectual communication. Soon she returned, book open, pages flying until she found the passage that would illustrate her point.

"'The purpose of life is not to be happy.'" Thumping at each word with one finger, she read on. "'It is to be *useful*, to be *honorable*, to be *compassionate*; to have it make some difference that you have lived, and lived well.' That's what I'm trying to say. Besides, happiness is only momentary—it's nothing you can count on."

"I don't believe that. There are happy people and unhappy people. You used to be an unhappy person. Now you seem more like a happy person to me," I argued, wishing my mother could answer a simple personal question and talk to me about how she felt.

"Yes, I admit I'm happier now. But it can't be sustained like sunshine every day." Her protest came strong, as if she had to defend herself against my new law that everybody must live in a state of euphoria.

"Every day isn't sunny, Mother. I know that." I'd had enough of her preaching and walked away, leaving her alone with Mr. Emerson. After one of Mother's philosophical discussions, I felt like someone had stomped around inside my head.

* * *

Almost before we were settled and with two more months before I would start my senior year, I auditioned for a part in a play at the Ojai Art Center. In Grand Junction I had grown up singing, even had voice and dance lessons, but Reggie had talked me out of trying out for the talent show at school.

"Why would you want to make a fool of yourself?" he said. "It will take up too much of your time, and I'm not going to wait around for you."

This meant he would break up with me and I would be alone. I had already given up my friends for him—not because he asked me to in so many words, but because he wanted all my time—and all other activities except for school that did not involve the back seat of his car.

As for the world premiere of *Wind from the Sea* at the Art Center, it was in answer to the 1950s age of conformity. It is a rule that when the pendulum swings too far in one direction, it must swing back. *Wind from the Sea* was playwright Steven Lackner's contribution to the *avant garde*. "Set at a carnival near the sea of no identifiable country, each of the nine scenes dealt with a part of man's universal search for the meaning of life," the newspaper said. As the magician's assistant, I had no lines. But as a peasant girl in one of the crowd scenes, I rushed ahead of the crowd to give the alert. "Look! He's coming over the hill!"

We rehearsed three nights a week, and because I was only in a few scenes, I spent hours sitting out front listening to the director and watching the principal actors rehearse. The play itself was full of nuance and deep mystical meaning. I had no idea what was going on but sat riveted as the actors swept across the stage in flowing rehearsal capes and skirts. The newspaper story said the playwright, born in Paris to German parents, had novels, plays, and musical compositions to his credit. I figured that in some circles he was famous and that even though I didn't understand the play, it must be good. Having grown up with an artist—a mother I hardly ever understood—I knew there was a whole world of knowledge for me to grow into.

Backstage, two dressing rooms with racks of costumes waited for the actors. Actresses poured my first cup of black coffee. I studied my image in the lighted mirror and learned how to brighten my skin with makeup, line my eyes, highlight my cheekbones, and paint darker, more voluptuous lips for the stage lights.

The theatre people were mostly Mother's generation, artists and intellectuals with day jobs. They spoke with broad theatrical accents, used dramatic gestures—even during our monthly business meetings. I don't remember why I came to hold a position on the board. Most mysterious was their eagerness to teach, their openhandedness, their fondness for me, the ingénue.

In the years to come, I would dance and sing, laugh and cry on cue in every corner of that hardwood stage with the trap door. I would send my voice off across rows of uplifted faces to the man in the last row, make people laugh, and delight in curtain calls. When the door to the theatre opened for me, I walked through and felt truly at home.

*   *   *

At Nordhoff High School, I was shown into the principal's office. Horace H. Wilbur sat behind a desk with his back to a windowsill jungle of houseplants. Probably in his early fifties, he looked to me like a cross between Humphrey Bogart and Dagwood Bumstead. Dressed in a suit, vest, and tie, he wore his shock of thick dark hair slicked back and parted on the left. He welcomed me, directing me to sit in the chair that faced his big wooden desk. Glancing over my transcript from Grand Junction, he asked if I wanted to go to college.

"Yes," I said, without thinking. I was entering my senior year, and my parents hadn't mentioned college yet.

He picked up a tiny note pad and wrote my schedule of classes by hand.

"Tell me about Colorado—Grand Junction—what's it like there?"

"It's beautiful," I said, my face all lit up. "A mountain valley surrounded by the most beautiful mountains you can imagine."

"If you want to be well-liked at your new school," he interrupted, "forget about Grand Junction. Don't even think about it. You are here now. Your new friends don't want to listen to you moan and groan about all you left behind." He studied me a moment, as if to ask, "Am I being too rough?" I had held up under his onslaught of advice, and he leaned back in his chair. "I'm a firm believer that you'll get as much out of school as you are willing to put in. You know that while everyone is kneaded out of the same dough, we are not baked in the same oven. No—we—are—not!" He leaned abruptly forward. "You know, I always give this one little word of advice especially to the girls—a closed mouth catches no flies. Don't be a gossip. A rumor goes in one ear and out many mouths. Don't get your mouth involved."

Ready to open my mouth to agree, I nodded my head instead.

"Work hard in school, and remember if you believe everything you read you'd better not read." After a good laugh at his own joke, he regained his composure. "That's about all the advice I'm going to give you today." He stood up. "Take into account that good advice is annoying—bad advice never is. If I've been annoying that's all the more reason for you listen to what I've said. You can always come in to see me. I'll be right here."

"Thank you, Mr. Wilbur. I think I'm going to like this school."

"You may call me Poppa—Poppa Wilbur. That's what all my kids call me." He stood up and offered his hand. "You know, a tree always falls the way it leans." He smiled and looked me in the eye. "You look like a good girl to me."

No one had ever made me feel that I could succeed in school or that I was a good girl. I made a mental note to myself not to dream over Grand Junction in front of new friends, to never gossip, to study hard, and, most of all, to be the good girl Poppa Wilbur thought I was. I knew this was a tall order because I was a C student in Grand Junction where, at the age of fifteen, I had given away what was labeled "the most precious thing a girl has to give—her virginity." *Maybe here I could be good.*

The small high school occupied a one-story Spanish style stucco building with a red tile roof; two graceful old trees shaded the front lawn. There were only eighty-five kids in the senior class. On the first day of school I was nervous and felt out of place. I saw my sister Susan—who was entering her freshman year—down the hall struggling to open her locker. I can see her still, wearing a summer dress the color of a ripe peach. I wasn't good yet, so I didn't go to help her.

At lunchtime, as I walked around with my sandwich looking for a place to sit down, an attractive girl approached from across the lawn.

"Hi, Karen, I'm Anne." She had a big smile on her face and said, "Come have lunch with us."

She led me across the lawn to the shade and introduced me to her friends. There, six or more girls, all smiling, welcomed me to sit with them. I wondered how Anne knew my name. Years later, she told me that Poppa Wilbur had asked her to befriend me.

* * *

In Grand Junction, we attended the First Congregational Church. Even though Mother greatly admired the Reverend George Perkins, she wouldn't take the next step and join his church. That was a matter of principle. Mother wasn't a joiner.

I regularly attended youth group meetings with kids my age, but when Reverend Perkins asked me to join the church, Mother was alarmed.

"You don't want to be a joiner," she said, as if it would drive another nail in my conformist coffin. I didn't join because Mother said that joiners don't think for themselves. It didn't occur to me to take her advice, think for myself, and join the church. But if it had, I would not have had the strength of character to withstand her disappointment and scorn.

In Ojai, I became a joiner. Anne and her best friend Sandy belonged to Future Homemakers of America and the Drama Club. I joined too. My first social invitation came from Anne—a swimming party at her home. Both Anne and Sandy had beautiful swimming pools. Both were expert swimmers and divers—better than me.

Raymond, the captain of the football team and student body president, asked me to the FHA fair. We bought tickets for the cake raffle and, like magic, I won. I cut the gooey coconut cake with a plastic knife and shared it with all of Ray's friends hoping they would be my friends too.

Just when I believed I had been dropped off in paradise, Anne and Sandy got me a job modeling with them at Orchid Town Guest Ranch. At rehearsals one of the older models taught us how to do the model walk: hold shoulders back, suck in stomach, tip hips forward, put one foot down in front of the other, lengthen neck, and smile. I was lucky that in junior high, Mother had made me walk while balancing a book on my head. "You want to glide," she would say.

Fashionably dressed guests lunched and sipped wine at tables under umbrellas, a chamber orchestra played, and I strutted with my friends around the swimming pool modeling a brand new fashion, Bermuda shorts. We rushed back into the dressing room, changed, and emerged again in different outfits. I thought all the clothes were very smart. I was used to making my own clothes and decided to copy the elegant black sheath dress.

I studied and did my homework on time and almost never thought about being dumb.

Ray asked me out on several dates. I thought maybe I had a boyfriend, but the last time I went out with him he got "fresh." While kissing me goodnight one of his hands found my breast. Maybe he was just putting the new girl to the test. I reacted with alarm, pushed him away, and when he called again, I wasn't home.

From then on, whenever he saw me, he lowered his eyes or looked away embarrassed.

All seniors were required to take Poppa Wilbur's Senior Class, designed to prepare his students for life after high school. Sharing his homespun wisdom, he discussed marriage—mentioning his beloved wife—marriage's most common problems (without mentioning sex), and his redemptive life experiences.

"There, but for the grace of God, go I."

He said it often, teaching his kids to look at the adversity in other people's lives. We learned how to balance a checkbook, plan a household budget. All practical things. He told us that we should never "let the sun set" on anger toward anyone in our family and liked to say that the class of '56 was the best class he'd ever taught. We believed him.

In October, I walked out on the high school stage to audition for the leading role in the senior class play, *The Night of January 16th* by Ayn Rand. I landed the role of Karen Andre, a woman on trial for the murder of her wealthy boss. In November, I applied to Colorado Women's College in Denver. Mother had agreed that I should go to college and was able to talk my father in paying for it.

I had the hope that at last I could finally become the daughter my mother had always wanted.

During a general assembly, the whole school saw the first performance of the senior class play. On Friday night, we performed for the town. The first few minutes on stage I was so scared that I nearly froze until I spotted Mother, Susan, and Gretchen third row center and saw their smiles. I remembered my lines and my business, and I disappeared. Who I was trying so hard to be then and who I had been in Grand Junction vanished.

Afterwards, everyone heaped the cast with praise. "Some people just shine on stage—and you shine, Karen!" That's what my mother said. Some of the kids nicknamed me "Star."

A positive review in the school newspaper confirmed what I had come to believe. I would be an actress and like my Aunt Mary, who went to the Pasadena Playhouse to study drama, I would go to Colorado Women's College to begin my life on the stage. No one pointed out that if you want to study drama, there's a big difference between the Pasadena Playhouse and Colorado Woman's College.

I knew I was born for the stage; there was something lofty and noble about the legitimate theatre. Still, I admitted to myself alone that if the best I could do was the movies, I'd settle.

* * *

John Turner lived in an old house on Ojai Avenue, next door to his widower father's gas station. He was tall and good-looking—like Elvis Presley with a crew cut. Johnny knew his smile made my heart do flip-flops. All he had to do was gaze into my eyes and give me one of his sexy Elvis smiles and I felt lovely waves of excitement run all the way through me and come out of my mouth in giggles. Most of our dates were to basketball games, or the movies, and school dances.

By that time we were all dancing to rhythm and blues and very early rock and roll. At high school dances they spun platters—our favorite songs from the hit parade. There was a whole lot of shakin' goin' on at the Nordhoff gym. Our feet flew over the floor as Little Richard banged his way through "Tutti Frutti" and Bill Haley and The Comets rocked their version of "Shake Rattle and Roll." And when Johnny took me into his arms and they dimmed the lights, earth angel and the boy in the blue suede shoes moved like blue velvet to "All I Have to do is Dream," dream, dream.

I danced in my dreams after a date with Johnny. His kisses were sweet and he never ventured any farther. He told me I was too good for him. That I was the nicest girl he had ever dated and he wanted to show me that he knew how to treat me, a nice girl.

For the school talent show, Johnny and I did an old fashioned jitter-bug with all the twists and throws to "Rock Around the Clock." Poppa Wilbur called me into his office. "I hear you've been going out with John Turner. He's not the kind of boy I'd expect a nice girl like you to date. His background is very different from yours—he has a bad reputation."

Even though Anne had asked me about Johnny and I knew he wasn't on the approved list, I was surprised and came to Johnny's defense. "He's a nice guy. He treats me better than some boys." I was riled up enough that I leveled with Poppa. "When I first came to

Nordhoff, Ray asked me out. I had to stop dating him because he got fresh! Johnny has been a perfect gentleman!"

Wilbur's eyes widened, his jaw dropped. Ray was a student leader and one of Poppa's favorites. "Well, Karen," he said, dimly, "I am surprised, but I trust your judgment."

"Once people start talking about you, it's so hard. Johnny can't help what people say about him."

"That's true. Evil is sooner believed than good," he said earnestly, leaning across his desk. "I'm glad to hear a nice girl like you say something kind about John. He's got a reputation for being wild—though he's never been in any real trouble that I know of. You know, Karen, a wise man makes his own decisions; an ignorant man follows public opinion."

* * *

I'd learned how to study and my grades were As and Bs. I almost never thought about being dumb anymore—except for worrying about the SAT for college. In preparation, I took the dumbbell math class, designed to re-teach the basics to students faltering in math. My worst subject became one of my favorites. There was something completely liberating about being in a class where everyone else was dumb too.

That spring, I prepared for the Lion's Club Speech Contest. All the seniors in speech class had to write a speech to fit the title: *Youths' Problems of Tomorrow.* First everyone gave their talks in class. I was selected best speaker and sent as the representative from Nordhoff to speak against the winners from other schools. My toes curl now when I read the speech I gave in front of an audience of middle-aged Lions.

My premise: juvenile delinquency, low moral standards, racial segregation, and Communism were the problems youth faced. Communism was the common link—my conspiracy theory. I advocated sex education by parents and warned about Communists corrupting our youth. I spoke about the "few" young people who use "narcotics." But I admitted that not all "dope peddlers" were Communists. My solution to all of these problems was the spiritual transformation of the individual. We should "develop ourselves spiritually to the point where we are equal to our scientific and technological advancements. Then we will have no communism in America."

A boy from Thatcher School and another boy from Villanova (both posh prep schools) spoke against me. The boy from Villanova won, but I got a check for $5.00 and a Certificate of Appreciation.

* * *

After a date with Johnny, he'd pull his car into the driveway on Shady Lane. We'd sit there in the dark and kiss, the porch light gleaming in the near distance. My mother always gave us about fifteen minutes before she clicked the front porch light off and on in a frantic SOS meaning, "Get in the house this minute!" I'd give Johnny one last big kiss, then he'd walk me to the front door for one more last big kiss.

One night my mother must have been asleep at the switch because we had more time than usual. Even the windows were steamy. "I'd better go in."

"I have to tell you something first," Johnny said, unwilling to let me out of his arms. "Sometimes after a date with you—after sitting like this with you in the car—I stop at Roberta's on my way home."

"Roberta's? What for?"

"For—you know—sex. I can't be like this with you—you drive me crazy."

I felt my hand shoot for the door handle.

"You're a nice girl. It's my way of not pressuring you."

"But—what about Roberta? Does she love—do you love her?"

"No—she means nothing—just fun. She wants to date me, but she knows it's hopeless because of you."

I knew Roberta. Her ears were pierced and she ran around with the wild crowd. I sat there a moment, thinking. Johnny was quiet too. I felt sorry for Roberta and disappointed in him. I wished Johnny hadn't told me, that he hadn't made it sound like he was doing me a favor. I would keep Roberta's secret, even from Sandy and Anne. I knew all about the shame she felt.

There, but for the grace of God, go I.

12

Nice Girl

1955

WHEN I WAS very young, I wanted to be a cowgirl. But, by the time I was in junior high school I wanted to be a minister's wife. In high school I'm not sure I thought of being anything but a wife and mother. In Ojai, girls had boyfriends but they also had plans. Sandy wanted to be a professional golfer, and Anne wanted to be a stewardess and travel the world. Back in Grand Junction, most of my friends wanted to get married. Until I came to life in Ojai, I'd blown around with the wind with no real awareness that I had choices. In the midst of Ojai magic, letters from my friends at home reminded me of my life there. Tammy, also seventeen, sent a newspaper clipping announcing her engagement to Sam, her high school boyfriend. It mentioned the dinner party given in their honor and listed the names of the guests—my friends. I felt the loss. I missed them and tucked the clipping inside my scrapbook for safekeeping.

How easy it had been to let Reggie lead me. For two years he'd planned my days and nights. Without all the temptations and drama of having a boyfriend, I was ready to play a new part. I wanted to be an actress and intellectual like my mother and that, in theory, meant being broad-minded. Except that also meant being discerning, which could easily slip into snobbery. She had helped me to hone my taste, to differentiate between high and low. We were not going to be ordinary because ordinary people didn't know how to think for themselves. I had finally boarded my mother's train. But, just like I'd sent Zackly away when I was small, I packed up my shame about the past and hid it. I would become the good girl I'd acted for my grandmother, the beautiful girl my father had wanted if he had to have a daughter at all, and the individual my mother could admire.

* * *

Daddy was engaged. He'd met Bonnie several years before on business trips to Denver. Mother confessed to us that for several years she had not been "a real wife" to him. We knew that meant she hadn't slept with him.

"I don't blame him for finding someone else," she said. "You should be happy he's found someone to love." It seemed all right to her. She made it sound logical and normal. It never occurred to us to look askance at either our father or our stepmother-to-be.

Before Christmas we returned to Grand Junction via a Greyhound bus—a long two-day overnight trip with stops for food and bathrooms. Three plane tickets were beyond our father's imagination. I have almost no memory of time spent with my family that Christmas. Our father and Bonnie weren't married yet, so we didn't meet her. I'm sure I spent time with my grandparents. I don't remember seeing my girlfriends. But I saved little mementos from nights out in Grand Junction: a wrapped sugar cube from Mark's Macongan, where our father took us to dinner, a book of matches from the Café Caravan, where I had dinner with Reggie.

Being with him again was like splitting in two: one side morphed into his girl, his thing; the other side broke off, rising free to Ojai. I tried to hold on to that side. When he'd called I'd hesitated before saying yes. But only for a moment.

Conversation over dinner with Reggie had never been memorable, but he asked me to go skiing after Christmas. Often, during my sophomore and junior winters, we had skied together in Aspen. Joy, Lonni, and Yvonne were going, and I could stay at their rooming house with them.

*   *   *

Aspen, in those days, was not a high-end ski resort. Mid-century it still showed its origins as an early silver mining town. At the elevation of 8,000 feet, the weathered old town filled with Victorian cottages and houses sat at the foot of Ajax Mountain, a world-class ski mountain almost 3,000 feet higher. I fell and broke my foot on that mountain my sophomore year and had to be rescued by the ski patrol. There were some bars and restaurants, a motel or two, and the old brick Hotel Jerome. A few privileged people lived in private ski lodges on the outskirts of town.

Cold and tired after a day on the slopes, my friends and I slipped our frozen feet into après-ski boots and headed for the Red Onion. We climbed into the dark pit by the fireplace with our boyfriends, anxious to get warm. Even though I was under age they served me all the beer I wanted. Reggie offered me a cigarette, and I lit up. We relived the day, laughing at each other's stories about our most spectacular and disastrous runs. Warmed by the closeness of the boys, the beer, and the crackling fire, we headed back to our rooms to shower and dress for dinner.

I pulled on the black sheath dress I had copied from the Orchid Town Guest Ranch fashion show, painted my lips red, clipped my mother's rhinestone earrings to my ears, and strung the matching choker around my throat. After dinner—in Reggie's car—my lips numb from booze and his kisses, my head woozy, I climbed into the back seat with him.

The next morning, a bruising headache and the taste of stale cigarettes and whisky reminded me of my shame. My poor mother had tried to teach me to think for myself, but when it came to Reggie I couldn't think at all. I had no power, no self-respect or confidence. I couldn't say no. And I couldn't say yes without self-loathing, guilt, and fear of pregnancy.

The following night, Reggie and I welcomed in the New Year together. At midnight we found ourselves surrounded by the noise and excitement of a crowded dance floor, music and noisemakers blaring, the cheers and crush of happy people, confetti falling like Technicolor snow. I embraced him and we wished each other a happy new year with a kiss. Everyone else in that crowded room looked happy.

"Come on, baby, let's go—I'll put the heater on in the car," he said, pulling me close, stroking my bottom with one hand.

"I can't. No."

"Why not?" He looked angry.

"Just scared," I said, "Let's dance." I didn't want him to be angry. "Let's just try and have fun dancing, like other people."

We bumped around among the dancers, out of step with the music, the mood, each other. He'd never cared for dancing.

"Let's have another drink."

"No thanks, I'm staying sober."

"You're coming outside with me." He yanked me toward the door by one arm.

"Please, Reg." I pulled away. "I'm afraid—" I hoped to arouse his sympathy. "You shouldn't want to take chances either."

"We took a chance last night," he said, tugging at my hand.

"We were stupid!"

His lips twisted, his eyes narrowed, he yanked me close, and through clenched teeth he whispered an old line in my ear: "Don't pretend you aren't a little whore."

I shuddered at his reminder, wishing I were safe on Shady Lane with my mother and sisters.

A friendly face appeared over Reggie's shoulder, a college boy smiling. He stopped and looked at me like he had just won the lottery, then took my hand and pulled me onto the dance floor. "You don't look so happy," he said, whisking me away to the music. He was a good dancer.

"My boyfriend—we aren't seeing eye-to-eye," I said, trying to be charming and jolly as Reggie left through the front door. As much as I wanted to be rid of him, I didn't know anyone at the party. I didn't want to be a pick-up.

"Well, maybe you and I can have some fun," he said. He still had that big friendly smile. He seemed like a nice boy. I must have asked his name. We danced well, but I knew it wasn't right to just pick up with a strange boy. I could not enjoy myself.

"I think your boyfriend is a fool."

"Thanks," I said, desperate to get away from him now and no idea how to do it.

"Hey, you really look upset. Would you like to go? I have my Jeep outside. I'll take you home."

We drove in his military-style Jeep through Aspen's snow-lit streets. Even in the dark, below the icy moon, I could see the majestic mountain towering above the valley and the lamp-lit streets full of old houses—most of them rather shabby. The college boy pulled up in front of our rooming house.

"Thanks, you really saved my life," I said, reaching for the door handle. I wasn't going anywhere. His arm was around me, his lips crashing against my teeth as his hand groped my breasts. "I don't feel well," I said, pushing him away. I was afraid to make him mad. "I feel really sick."

He threw his head back against the seat, groaned, flicked angrily at the car keys dangling from the dashboard, then opened his door. I put my hand on my door handle, but my father had taught me to wait. Like a gentleman, the college boy was coming to open the door.

As we walked up the shoveled walkway toward the front door, I thanked him again for the ride. The porch light was on, and I touched the doorknob. He grabbed me, spun me around, stuck his tongue in my mouth, and thrust his hand under my skirt.

Desperate, I moaned, let myself go limp and crashed like a dead woman onto a bank of snow. I lay there a moment in as fine a faint as had appeared on any stage in the world, snowflakes melting in my ears as my head warmed a pillow of snow. I wondered how long I would have to play dead before I could convincingly come to.

Bending near, his "Jeezus, are you okay?" hit the cold air.

It seemed safe to moan and flutter my eyelids. He helped me up, but before he could force himself on me again I cried, "I'm going to vomit."

"Jeezus!" he yelped, stepping back, and I escaped into the house.

The girls were still awake and tipsy, talking about their dates. When they asked, I told them what had happened. They all fell over laughing. After my girlfriends had gone to sleep I lay awake worrying, hating myself, wishing I were in Ojai where I was good. I wondered if all great actresses had learned their craft in high school, where survival depended upon a convincing performance.

13

Mother Turns Forty

1955

"What is a woman? I assure you, I do not know ... I do not believe that anybody can know until she has expressed herself in all the arts and professions open to human skill." —Virginia Woolf

EVEN IF YOU didn't count Mother's daily yoga practice in the garden or her peculiar mostly vegetarian diet—carrot juice, yoghurt, wheat germ, and sandwiches made of peanut butter, honey, and banana or, her very favorite, apple and cheddar on the driest, hardest, brownest bread she could find—my mother was not a traditional homemaker. At a time when nobody ate like that and nobody did yoga, my mother could wrap her legs around her neck and stand on her head. She taught herself how from a book. She was forty years old and divorced. In celebration of the new decade she'd just entered, she went down to the local photographer's studio and had her portrait made.

Our father sent enough for us to live moderately well. It had never entered our minds that Mother should go to work. She'd never worked, except briefly before marriage as a bank teller. Even that sounded fantastic to me. *My mother counting other people's money.* Somehow, we knew that to report daily to a job was impossible for her. She wasn't like Nana Pearl or her sister, Dorothy—they knew how to be in the world. Except for typing, I can't think of a single practical, or should I say money-making, thing mother could do. She had neither been offered nor sought a formal education and was unprepared for a career in any field that might interest her. Though no one had ever said so, we all knew that she just wasn't made for the real world. Besides, she did the strangest things.

One day Mother appeared with her arm in a sling.

"What's wrong with your arm?"

Her face lit up. "Oh, nothing. It's just a reminder."

"About what?"

"Well, I don't know if you've noticed, but my forehead is covered with bruises because I keep forgetting to close the kitchen cupboard doors and then I bang my head on them."

I hadn't noticed. I took a look at her battered forehead.

"This," she said raising her arm, and as if it should be perfectly obvious, "reminds me to close the cupboard doors."

Mother also appeared to have strange powers over household objects. Frequently, when she walked into the cluttered kitchen a glass or a spoon would fly off the counter and crash to the floor. She would panic, hold her hands up, palms out, and exclaim that she hadn't touched anything—and she hadn't.

In a day when things like socks were darned (the old art of reweaving a hole with needle and thread) and broken toasters were taken to a repairman, Mother just threw them out. My sisters and I thought that was scandalous.

Early in the morning, while getting ready for school, we could hear our mother working in the kitchen. She was making breakfast. Cupboard doors slammed, pots were shuffled here and there, drawers opened and shut and opened and shut, and maybe a plate would clatter and fall into the sink. Something was burning. The whole kitchen was torn apart. Finally, she sat down at the kitchen table with a cup of black coffee and a plate with one piece of burnt toast. She liked it that way. We ate the oatmeal she'd made or cold cereal from a box, which was fine with us.

The strangest moment of all came in a letter she wrote me after I was married. She triumphantly described the adventure she'd had that day. Just outside the front door, she found a rattlesnake coiled and ready to strike the moment she opened the door. She fashioned a weapon by lashing a long-handled fork to a mop handle. Then she opened the door, raised her lance, stepped forward, and lunged at the snake's head, stabbing it just where the head and neck met. She didn't give details about the snake bleeding or writhing to its painful end, but she was thrilled with herself.

Even later, Mother wrote that her car had died and she had killed it. "The dashboard light came on and it was green. I thought that meant *go*." She kept going and soon discovered that the light had been a warning. Her car needed oil and she burned up her engine. She was never able to afford a car again and for the rest of her life walked everywhere.

In Ojai, Mother didn't go to church any more. That meant we didn't either. The world appeared large and new, filled with endless possibilities. The church suddenly seemed old hat. The people and institutions Mother had known all her life were back in Grand Junction. There was no social circle, no small town society to worry about, and she had become an apostate. Mother wrote and read philosophy—books by Bertrand Russell and Albert Schweitzer—taking longer and longer detours with her spiritual guru Jiddu Krishnamurti.

*   *   *

On a blanket in the park shaded by a large live oak, Mother and I waited. We had come into a gathering of Krishnamurti's followers. This was not my idea, but I was curious so I said yes when she asked me to come with her. A man of sixty, Krishnamurti had given talks to seekers since both he and the century were in their twenties. When he began to speak, his voice was light but deep. His accent was thick, but he spoke slowly in order to be understood. Luckily for me, he was fascinating to look at—white hair, extraordinarily beatific face, and rich brown skin covered by his flowing white shirt and pants.

As he spoke, he said something like this. "Freedom is not a reaction; freedom is not choice. It is man's pretense that because he has choice he is free. Freedom is pure observation without direction, without fear of punishment and reward. Freedom is without motive; freedom is not at the end of the evolution of man but lies in the first step of his existence—"

My eyes glazed over and I thought I might be sitting on a pebble. I shifted around a bit but couldn't get comfortable. Wishing I could lie down and close my eyes, I looked around at rapt faces. Everyone was sitting with open eyes holding their breath.

"Freedom is found in the choiceless awareness of our daily existence—"

What is he talking about?

I looked at my spellbound mother. Then there were trees to look into, twisted limbs, sun sparkles dancing in the breeze, a squirrel doing tricks, birds coming and going. I decided to look around stealthily to see if I could find someone who might possibly become a friend for Mother. Someone who could go with her to Krishnamurti talks and other boring events. Mother had made no effort to meet people or find new friends. She wasn't unfriendly, I was sure of that. I believe that for years she had longed for time alone when she could paint, write, read, or meditate. Finding that in Ojai, she wasn't ready to let it go.

In Grand Junction, I'd heard Mother and her friends comment about women's tendency to gossip, and their preoccupation with housework. They took pride in never mentioning their female troubles, childbirth, and child rearing—all things unworthy of their thoughts and certainly not topics for discussion. These women were all creative people, including a Martha Graham–trained dancer, a painter, a pianist. All were women who liked to read the books Mother read. You couldn't call them feminists. They didn't go that far. My guess is that they were prejudiced against their own sex.

Not long after we settled in Ojai, Mother made a workspace for herself in her bedroom and went to work on a novel. She had attended a two-week writer's workshop in the Berkshire Mountains the summer before we left Grand Junction. She came home from the "lush green" Massachusetts hills excited; the writers she met there stimulated and encouraged her, and she received positive feedback from her teachers. By the time she arrived in California, she had come up with the plot for a novel.

She wrote faithfully every day while we were at school and sometimes in the evenings. In anticipation of her novel being published, she drew a picture with pen and ink: a bird sitting on an egg in a nest with "Just hatched" inscribed underneath. She explained that writing a book is like an egg pecked slowly away from inside so a living thing may emerge.

Her book was about the life and career of an architect named David; her protagonist was a man, not a woman. I wondered if he looked like the statue of Michelangelo's beautiful David we had seen in Mother's art books. I asked if she had the Biblical story of young David in mind. She said that her David, through faith in himself and not the Old Testament God, kills a metaphorical giant.

She guarded her story like a military secret and would not let me read a word. She wouldn't even talk about it or answer questions.

"If I talk about it, I won't write it." That was her deep-felt conviction.

I was able to weasel enough information that I came to believe that David was Mother's dream of a perfect man.

She had already described the kind of man I should look for in a husband. She called him a soul mate. Under the influence of my mother, popular song lyrics, and all the romance I witnessed in the movies, I formed a detailed picture of the only man worthy of my love. Because he loved me I wouldn't have to ask for what I wanted; he would know what would make me happy. If a man wanted to make love to me, it was because he *loved* me. My job was to be beautiful and loving and create a comfortable home where he would find rest. His job was to take care of me and protect me from the world.

Mother added a few more requirements: while he thought about toweringly important things—the high arts and philosophy—so would I. I wouldn't have to be in the world where he lived fully and richly, but—and this is important—his mastery over worldly things would allow him to be healthily detached from material things. In other words, he would be a spiritual man.

I was supposed to keep my eyes open for a man like that and marry him.

Though Mother never said ugly things about my father, somehow she conveyed that he was lacking. He was not a bad man, but deficient and dull, his interests trivial. And though she said none of this in so many words, I could see that he was an ordinary, boring man. Mother, on the other hand, was his opposite. She conveyed that also.

After months of hard work, Mother had a revelation.

"I've made a decision—I think I'm too isolated."

"How do you mean?"

"Well, there's more to writing than long hours at the typewriter. A writer should be in the middle of real life, with real people. I should get out more—talk to people—so I can see how they interact with one another, how they move and talk."

It sounded like a good idea to me. "Why don't you go to the Art Center? Maybe you could be in a play or work backstage. There are some real people there."

For the Art Center's production of *The Rainmaker*, she designed a beautiful model of the small half-house that was eventually built on a revolving platform. Her work was elegant in its detail, brilliant even to my eyes. But once the play was over, Mother went back to her typewriter. Except when a new play opened at the Art Center, or Krishnamurti gave a talk in the park, or she could do one of the other things she liked to do in Ojai like going to the Folk Dance Festival or driving up the mountain to visit Beatrice Wood's studio, she seldom ventured out.

What happened?

At the cast party after opening night of *The Rainmaker*, while standing in line at the buffet table talking to some of the cast, a man came up behind Mother and put his hand on her bottom.

She stabbed him with her fork.

Then one day I came home from school to find my mother worried and frightened. Her good friend's husband had called long distance from Grand Junction.

"You won't believe who called this morning—Tom Houghton—Margaret's husband."

"How's Tom and Margaret?"

"I didn't ask," she said looking bewildered. "Do you know what he had the nerve to say to me? That he'd always been in love with me. He asked me if I wanted him to come out here—and if I did, he said he'd be on the first plane."

I was shocked. "What did you say?"

"I was so stunned I didn't know what to say."

"You must have said something."

"Well, yes, I must have—I just remember—something, of course, like Margaret being a dear friend and that I thought he'd sunk pretty low. I can't tell you how disgusted—frightened I've been all day. You don't think he'd come here anyway, do you?"

I didn't know, but I said he wouldn't just to get her to calm down.

In the days that followed Mother jumped every time the phone rang. She would ask Susan and me to answer. When she was alone she let the phone ring while she took a walk. Sometimes she just took it off the hook.

Mother wasn't able to laugh off these incidents with men. She stabbed a man with a fork. As she told me a year before, on that night in Grand Junction when we were alone in my dark room, "When I was your age I was raped." I was the only person on earth that she had told. She had kept her secret and never sought psychological help. Submitting to psychoanalysis just wasn't done by the middle class. Nobody even used the word *therapy* unless it related to the physical. The very idea would have brought up the insane asylum: visions of men in white coats, patients with blank stares, and screams in the night.

14

Melodrama

1956 – 1957

Melodrama: Finds its source in plot rather than character. It is characterized by sensational incidents, contrived situations, and accidental solutions. Usually serious.—Karen Vorbeck, note in her Composition and Rhetoric notebook

ON MY WAY to Denver and my freshman year in college, I stopped in Grand Junction to see my father and meet his new wife. Bonnie's salt and pepper hair, her face round as a peach, didn't conform to my image of a seductress who had lured my father away. Still her hair was fashionably styled, her makeup tastefully done, her dress strikingly smart, her jewelry expensive—the engagement ring platinum with, I'm guessing, close to one-carat diamonds on either side of the big sparkling rock in the middle.

When I hugged him hello at the airport, the sight of father and daughter in an embrace drove Bonnie to retrieve a Kleenex from her sleeve and wipe tears of happiness from her eyes. On the drive home she asked about school, congratulated me for selecting Colorado Women's College, and seemed delighted by my ambition for a career on the stage. She adored the theatre, she said, and joked that once I hit the big time she would be front row center. It was impossible not to notice that Bonnie wanted to make a good impression, and that endeared her to me.

Bonnie's starry-eyed, adoring gazes at my father did not go unnoticed. Mother had never looked at him like that—not that I'd seen. I remembered Mother's words. "Don't blame your father for the end of this marriage. I haven't been a wife to him in years."

The moment we entered the house I noticed that the new furnishings and the art were not Mother's taste. My father didn't go in for home decoration, so Bonnie must have made the changes. During the cocktail hour, Bonnie matched Daddy drink for drink, and appearing sober, bustled over the preparation of food. Declining my offer of help in either the kitchen or dining room, she set the table with placemats and linen napkins.

It felt strange—eating at the dining table Mother designed and had built. The drapes had not changed, but a large new oil painting loomed over the table, executed by a skilled fine-art painter. Bonnie explained that it was a wedding gift from friends whose son had painted it while confined to a mental institution. By the time I finished half my spaghetti, its presence troubled me. The sad clown sat fully costumed inside a kiddie pool in a puddle of water with tears streaming from his eyes. Water, I wondered aloud, or was it tears?

"No! It's water," my father said.

*   *   *

I'd traveled by train to Denver with my grandmother but had never made the trip alone. The train followed the Colorado River through the foothills, then climbed to higher elevations with alpine meadows and mountain scenes before it descended into Denver. I had plenty of time to read and to think about Daddy and his new wife. *What would Mother think of Bonnie?* I liked her. As the years went by— though they seldom met—Daddy's two wives had friendly relations.

The school sent a station wagon to the depot to pick me up. Except for the small black and white picture at the top of the school's brochure, I'd never seen the campus. We pulled up to expansive lawns shaded by beautiful old trees framing a series of graceful brick buildings. The driver stopped in front of my dorm. Foote Hall, the rambling three-story building with gables, looked like an English manor house to me. I felt as if I were being dropped off in a foreign country. As I marched up the long walk toward the front door, the driver following with my luggage, I remembered my grandmother's advice. "A college education is important. A well-bred girl must be prepared to speak knowledgably with her husband and his business associates." Only five percent of women went to college during the fifties—and most who did were in search of a successful husband. There was a popular saying: I'm off to get my MRS degree.

In the dormitory office, a large fiftyish woman wearing a gray suit waited behind a desk. Greeting me with a forced smile, the house mother looked like she'd been sent by central casting. Crossing me off the roster, she gave me the key to room 222.

"You may call me Miss Bukowski."

Eleanor Holbrook from Cheyenne, Wyoming, my roommate, had already checked in. We had exchanged letters over the summer. I knew Eleanor would study accounting and was engaged.

No one was home in room 222, but Eleanor had unpacked. She made up the bed by the window, set her things on the desk she wanted, and neatly hung her clothes in her closet. That made it simple. I took the other bed, desk, and closet. When Eleanor arrived, she looked exactly like the senior class picture she'd sent in one of her letters—clean-cut with a dark red ducktail, dark red lipstick, and an air that said, "I'll make an efficient and skillful legal secretary."

Our room was one of two in a suite divided by a short hall and the bathroom we would share with suite-mates in room 220. One sink, one bathtub, and one toilet for four girls.

Right off, suite-mate Sylvia, a liberal arts major from Nebraska, seemed a little overbearing. I knew I didn't want her for an enemy. But figured I was safe when Sylvia smiled and said, "I'm gonna call you Becky." Puzzled at first—I'd never had a nickname—I realized she had created Becky from my last name. Sylvia's roommate, tall, glamorous Margot from Beverly Hills, would study fashion design.

Once we settled in, the chemistry among suite-mates became awkward. Sylvia, Margot, and I were finally on our own, away from home for the first time, eager for a little adventure. Eleanor was prissy, a stick-in-the-mud, a party pooper. Still, she was my roommate and I tried my best to be friendly and tidy and not let Eleanor's perfected discipline annoy me.

Every day when I came in after class, I found her studying. While waiting for Sylvia and Margot to come home, I studied too. Eleanor went early to bed and was early to rise. She seemed already grown up, living her life on schedule, doing everything in boring moderation. She had trained her fiancé to call long distance every other night at 8:30, and they would talk until 8:35.

On the other hand, Sylvia buried the telephone receiver in her pillow and fell asleep every night with her boyfriend breathing in her ear. Sylvia could hardly be civil to Eleanor. Margot avoided her, and I spent most of my spare time in room 220 or the smoker down the hall where the girls played bridge and smoked a blue haze over the room.

My English teacher, Miss Holloway, gave me high marks. I loved writing and reading the assigned books. When I wrote my parents about my delight in school, Mother wrote back. "You've discovered the sacred process of learning. How wonderful you are." Daddy's letter mentioned the weather back in Grand Junction and the news that he would take Bonnie on vacation to New Orleans.

I struggled with French and found psychology fascinating as I looked for symptoms in everyone including myself. I felt favored in the drama department with Miss Butler. There I got to do scenes from plays and, in acting class, pretended I was a tree in a wind storm and a boulder resting alongside a busy highway. Theatre director Horace Latimer looked for plays with all-female casts, imported a few male guest stars, or did something fun like a melodrama in which tall girls lowered their voices and played men.

Etiquette, social graces, and something close to old-fashioned elocution were taught by Miss Livingston. While sitting through the beautiful young modeling instructor's lectures, I began to suspect that the class had been designed to help us catch a husband and become model wives. Miss Livingston's demonstrations were extremely helpful. She pulled a chair to the front of the class and modeled the proper way to sit: how to scoot a little forward, cross the legs at the ankles, and pull them to one side at a graceful angle.

She demonstrated how to smoke like a lady. Reaching for a pack of cigarettes, she removed the cigarette, tapped one end of it gently on the table, struck a match while holding the cigarette between her right index and middle fingers, and lit up. She crossed her legs properly, inhaled, and languorously blew out the smoke. Lauren Bacall couldn't have done it better.

"Never, never hold a cigarette between your thumb and index finger and never let it dangle from your lips." We all laughed at her imitation of a sudden slouch and dangling cigarette.

Miss Livingston read a list of area colleges and the income brackets of their male graduates. Out of all the schools, the young men from Colorado School of Mines would make the wealthiest husbands. I had just met Roberto from the Colorado School of Mines and made no objection, but wondered if this was the right thing to teach girls.

What about love?

Dorm rules were strict. Except for fathers, men were not allowed in the girls' rooms. When fathers came to visit (mine never did), warning shouts rang in the halls. "Man in the hall! Man in the hall!" came punctuated with the sound of doors slamming. Miss Bukowski made unannounced room checks to see if the girls kept their rooms clean—their bathrooms scoured bright. We were not allowed to smoke, drink alcohol (ever), or play poker in our rooms.

* * *

On a Saturday night during Thanksgiving vacation, when the dorm was almost empty, Sylvia, Margot, and I decided to break all the rules. Eleanor, the only sensible person in the suite, had gone home to Cheyenne. Sylvia asked her of-age boyfriend to buy us a bottle of booze. As a joke he showed up with a half-gallon of 100 proof grain alcohol. Margot bought two large bottles of grape juice for mix. We already had cigarettes and cards and pockets full of nickels and dimes. As a matter of principle, we were going to play a forbidden game: *poker*.

We invited Joy and Edie from 217. They were freshmen too. Joy was a friendly blonde from New Mexico. I envied her pageboy. Tiny, dark Edie lived on a ranch in Wyoming.

Bravely, we gathered cross-legged in a circle on the floor. A lit cigarette bouncing up and down as it dangled from her lips, Sylvia announced, "I'll deal. Becky, you pour."

Everyone held up the drinking glasses from their bathrooms, and I splashed three or so inches of grain alcohol into the bottom of each glass. Margot filled them with grape juice.

"Wish we had some ice."

"Hey, Edie, if you don't want Miss Bukowski making a surprise room check, we'd better lock the door."

Edie hopped up and ran to the door. "Did you hear? Bukowski caught Jean with a boy in her room last night."

"You're kidding! What'll they do to her?"

"She's already on her way home. We'll never see her again."

We sipped our drinks. "Hey, this isn't bad." The grape juice masked most of the alcohol taste, and the drink went down easy as Kool-Aid.

"We forgot to get something to eat."

"How did Jean get a boy past Miss Bukowski in the first place?"

We girls were used to coming home from our dates to a house mother standing sentry at the door. She looked us over carefully. Was the hair mussed, the lipstick smeared, alcohol on the breath?

"She's on the first floor. He climbed in through her window."

"You should have seen Bukowski trying to smell my breath last Saturday night." Sylvia laughed and downed the rest of her drink. "Filler 'er up, Becky." She handed over her glass. "Bud and I had been out to dinner and dancing and you know me. Bukowski acted like she was my best friend. She came up real close—'Did you have a good time, dear?'" she mimicked. "'Where did that nice young man take you tonight? Wasn't it a lovely evening—so warm for November?' Good thing I already popped a Sen-Sen."

Playing five-card draw, I lit another cigarette and poured drinks all around. "Sally told me Miss Holloway is having an affair with a senior girl," I blurted. "What on earth did she mean?"

"Some girls like girls," Sylvia said.

"What do you mean 'like girls'? An affair means sex, doesn't it?"

"Sex, yes. Sex. They do it together." Sylvia laughed at me.

"How?" I couldn't picture it.

"I'll be damned if I know. Do you know, Margot?"

"No. I guess you'll have to use your imagination."

"Do they like boys too?" I wondered.

"I'm quite sure they do *not*," Sylvia snipped as she claimed the pot. "That's why they're called lesbians." She ground her cigarette butt into the ashtray. "Please stop, Karen. You are so dumb."

"I'm not dumb!" Turning to Joy and Edie, I asked, "Have you ever heard of such a thing?"

"No!" they said in unison.

"See, they never heard of it either. I'm not dumb. We just don't have lesbians in California."

"Wanna bet? Now shut up and let me deal. Ante up," Sylvia barked. We threw nickels into the pot and with varying degrees of confidence revealed our hands.

When Edie won the pot with a full house, she burst into tears. "Oh, I can't believe it. I've never won anything before, not in my whole life, not ever, not even once ever," she sobbed. "They always beat me—my brothers and my Dad. I'm the worst player in the world, the worst, the pits, the . . ." Edie stopped herself, put her hand over her mouth, and ran for the bathroom.

We heard her vomiting and she cried, "Oh, my god," through the open door.

Sylvia threw her cards on the floor and ran to her aid. I felt queasy, and the sound of vomiting gave me the urge to vomit too. The rest of the girls had the same reaction and we raced for the bathroom.

Edie was sitting on the floor sobbing, clutching the toilet seat as Sylvia tried to comfort her. "It's okay, Baby," she said as the rest of us hurled purple vomit into the sink and bathtub.

"Oh, shit," Sylvia said, leaping up from the floor. She pushed me aside and heaved into the tub.

After the vomiting stopped, we lurched around the bathroom trying to clean up the mess. Finally, because of the stench, we decided to open the window, close the bathroom door, and finish up tomorrow.

We stumbled back into room 220 and sprawled on the beds and the floor. I felt a little better, but I was dizzy as a tilt-a-whirl and lay down on Margot's bed. The ceiling spinning overhead made me feel worse, and I had to sit up.

Sylvia had tiny Edie in her lap. She couldn't stop crying. "Now, Baby," Sylvia, slurred with a thick tongue, "you're going to be just peachy. You are a peach, isn't she, gals?" We all agreed that Edie was a peach.

"But I'm not. I'm a—if you knew about me—if you knew, you would never speak to me ever—never—ever again," she cried.

We all crawled to her side and put our hands out to touch our little friend. "We will too," we pledged.

"You can tell us anything, Edie. Anything."

"No matter what, we will still love you."

"What's wrong? Tell us what's wrong, Edie."

"He raped me. That's why I couldn't go home for Thanksgiving," she bawled. "He raped me! Now my mother won't let me back in the house." She sobbed and clutched at Sylvia. "What's going to happen to me? I can't go home."

"Who did that?" Margot demanded.

"My dad," Edie moaned. "He's always done bad things to me, but last time he—and Mother saw." She buried her face in Sylvia's neck and could not go on.

I was dumbstruck as was everyone else. None of us had ever heard of anything like that. Suddenly overcome with sadness I crawled away across the room and put my head on the edge of Margot's bed. Everyone grew terrifyingly silent; the only sounds Edie's shudders and gasps with tears.

Sylvia was the first to speak. "That bastard, how could he—his own daughter?" The rest of the girls didn't know what to say.

Edie pulled away from Sylvia and tried to stand, but slumped back on the bed. "See, I told you. Now they know and they hate me." She pointed at me and the others. "You all hate me. I can tell."

We all went to Edie's side and reached to touch her again. Joy climbed in bed beside them. I took her hand.

"No, we don't hate you."

"Poor Edie, try and go to sleep now."

"We will always be your friend."

*   *   *

According to one of Mother's good friends, the one place a girl could always find young men was at a woman's college—"They flock there." She had attended CWC years before and knew what she was talking about. The college held dances almost every weekend, and busloads of boys were brought in: cadets from the Air Force Academy and students from the University of Colorado, Colorado School of Mines, and Colorado State College.

Most of my dates were forgettable, except for Roberto, a student from the Colorado School of Mines. He was a senior from Colombia, the son of the president of Tikal Airlines. He was tall and manly, exotically handsome with a deep-voiced Spanish accent. His BMW convertible drove me into the mountains for a day of scenic wonders and to dinner and dancing at the best hotels and night spots. He even condescended to go slumming with me at the Windsor Hotel.

The old hotel was charged with Golden Age romance. In the ballroom, converted into a cabaret with a stage, old-fashioned melodramas like *Ten Nights in a Barroom* and *A Fate Worse Than Death* were performed. We were served beer and popcorn at a table with a red and white checkered tablecloth and a candle dripping wax over a Chianti bottle. Nationwide, Gay Nineties melodramas were all the rage back then. Just like theatre goers a hundred years before, the audience had fun booing and hissing the villain and cheering for the hero who rescued the poor, helpless, but always fair heroine. Roberto didn't seem to get *camp*. Old plays with sensational plots, stereotypical characters, and exaggerated acting did not make him laugh. That was disappointing.

I dated him for several months, puzzled by his passionless kisses, which contrasted starkly to the many stirring slow dances we shared on night club and hotel dance floors. He asked me to marry him, saying he would take me home to his wealthy parents.

"For the rest of your life, you will have servants and everything you want," he promised.

Flattered, I gave him a little "thank you kiss," but I didn't want to get married. I didn't love him.

"If I was going to marry anyone, Roberto, it would be you, but I can't marry you. I am going to be an actress." I had just landed the leading role in the school play—Lily Fairweather in *Lily the Felon's Daughter*, a melodrama written in the 1870s.

Roberto didn't call again.

*   *   *

In spring when the cherry and crabapple trees were blossoming on the campus lawn and the girls with money to spend made trips into downtown Denver to shop for summer clothes, my father called.

"How's the weather on that side of the mountain?"

"Nice," I said, wondering why he called. He'd never called before and was frugal enough not to waste money on a long distance call to chat about the weather.

"School is going to be over in a couple of months. I thought it only fair to let you know that I won't be sending you back to college next fall."

"Oh?" I didn't know what to say, but did ask, "Why?"

Silence.

"It's too expensive—and with your plane trips back and forth to California…"

Silence.

"Oh, I see."

"Besides, you don't need a college education. You can always get married."

"Uh."

Silence.

"Uh, I understand."

"Well, money doesn't grow on trees. I'll say goodbye now."

"Goodbye, Daddy."

I didn't know what to say, or how to argue my case. Later when I thought about it, I wished I had said something like, I'm doing well in school and I don't want to get married. If I'd wanted to be a doctor and a service to humanity, maybe I would have known what to say. But my dreams weren't noble. Becoming an actress did not sound important enough for his sacrifice. It sounded like a childish dream. Getting married sounded realistic.

In the answer to the letter I wrote Mother about my father's withdrawal of support, she didn't sound upset or outraged by my father's decision. Her stoic acceptance seemed to confirm that she thought I could get by without a college education, just like she had.

*   *   *

A headline in the *Rocky Mountain News* read, "CWC Will Present Lavish Melodrama." The *Denver Post* caption under my photograph said, "Stars as Lily." The *Grand Junction Daily Sentinel* ran a story under the headline "Former Resident to Play Lead in Play." I was most excited by the story in my hometown newspaper. *Now all my old friends know—maybe even Reggie.*

My character, Lily Fairweather, had a tragic beginning. Her mother died when she was an infant. Her father is a felonious, blackhearted scoundrel named Robin Steel. Act 1 opens in the Victorian parlor of a mansion in Boston's Beacon Hill. As Lily, I was costumed in a Gibson Girl blouse and long black skirt, looking pure as the driven snow in a blonde wig with ringlets and makeup exaggerated to produce innocent wide-open eyes and rosebud lips. From the Victorian maroon velvet sofa, Lily's adoptive mother tells her for the first time about the day she and her husband—while out for a stroll—saw a sign in a window: *Baby for Sale.* How she, as a mother who had lost her baby daughter to death, brought Lily home to raise as her own. Lily and Aunt Betsy put down their embroidery, embrace, and burst into heart-wrenching song: "For Sale—A Baby."

By act 3 the family fortunes have changed drastically, the Fairweathers are poor, and Lily has been disappointed in love by a craven coward. Then her gown is faded and tattered elegance in pink.

I had learned the broad theatrical gestures used at the turn of the nineteenth century and portrayed Lily's innocence and anguish with my own fraught desire to succeed in the role. My new boyfriend's eyes burned on me from the audience, but my father and Bonnie didn't come.

While the audience roared with laughter—and without a thought for my own situation—my Lily raised the back of her hand to her forehead, swooned, and cried, "Woe is me. Woe is me!"

15

Dramatis Personae

1957

Karen .... Herself
Willa Vinson .... Karen's Roommate
Robert Larson .... The Director
Lila Klingensmith .... Housemother
Jerry .... Photographer
Jared Kline .... Very Bad Boy
Dale Pace .... Handsome Actor
Loretta Gould .... Beautiful Actress
Bruce Payne .... Tab Hunter Look-alike
Dan Manchester .... Handsome Cop

WHILE I WAS still at CWC, someone sent me a classified ad from the *Los Angeles Times*, a casting call for a summer stock company on Santa Catalina Island off the coast of southern California. They were looking for young actors available to work for room and board. I sent a letter and picture of myself as Lily Fairweather and rather quickly received a reply requesting a tape recording of my voice.

Miss Nelson helped me tape a couple of Lily's monologues, and I mailed them to California. Soon theatre director Robert Larson sent congratulations. He wanted me in the troupe. Beside myself with joy, I ate nothing but buttermilk and bananas until I was thin.

* * *

Not long after my father told me he would not pay for any more college, I had convinced myself that this little set-back was unimportant. I did not allow myself more than a moment's pity. After years of training, I knew how to make everything fine. We didn't talk about my future or what lay ahead past summer, but after the Island Players accepted me, both my mother and I put our hopes in that. Maybe I'd be discovered. *They* might find me on Catalina Island—only a stone's throw from Hollywood—and make me a big star in the movies. I'd be rich and famous. I wouldn't have to be married and disappointed like my mother, or like Aunt Dorothy, whose husband had died and left her to support herself. I wouldn't have to be like Nana Pearl, who held on to worthless gold mine stocks and dreamed about her ship coming in. I'd fill my sails with wind from the sea, and my ship would race across the water.

That June, my mother and sisters drove me to the dock at Wilmington. To avoid the jumble of traffic and the crowds, she pulled the car to the curb about half a block from the bustling ferry terminal.

"Break a leg, Karen!" Susan called as I climbed out of the car.

"You'll get all the best parts!" Gretchen reached out to touch my hand.

As my mother and sisters bid me farewell, I could tell by the light in their eyes that they had big hopes for me.

* * *

Robert, a professor at one of the Los Angeles area colleges, had founded the Island Players in 1954. Shortly before the 1957 season began, he'd called his new troupe together in L.A. and had given us the script for *Camille, or Lady of the Camellias*, our first play. In short order, he'd cast the play (I got two small parts) and told us to learn our lines—to come to the island prepared for work. The troupe was made up of one middle-aged woman, five young women, and five young men. Right off I'd been drawn to one of the young women, a dancer with long black hair, exotic brown eyes, and ivory skin.

As I hurried toward the ferry terminal, there she stood, on the sidewalk just ahead.

"Hello," I called, out of breath. She turned to look at me and smiled in recognition. "I'm sorry," I said, "but I've forgotten your name."

"That's good because I've forgotten yours too." She laughed warmly. "I'm Willa Vinson."

I re-introduced myself, and before we could say another word we saw Robert Larson making a beeline our way. He was out of breath and sweating profusely. A large man, about forty-eight, his thin salt and pepper curls stood up in wild sweaty ringlets as his words came fast and wet.

"Howdy, gals! Where have you been?" he gushed. "The rest of us are over by the gangplank waiting for you."

I thought he was very unpleasant looking with his oversized stomach and misshapen, discolored teeth. Robert carried a large bundle, and huffing and puffing, he handed us sweat-splashed posters. "Carry these—hold them up so that everyone on board can see. It'll be good for business."

I looked at the poster.

1957
Fourth Smash Season
CATALINA PLAYERS
present theatre under the stars
at the Patio Theatre
EVERY NIGHT!
Beautiful girls! Handsome men!
$1.00

"You want us to carry these?" Willa sounded doubtful.

"Hold 'em up in front of you, lick your pretty lips, and smile!"

He pointed toward the gangplank and told us to join the others. Ordering his troupe to stick together, he moved us onto the boat, where he selected two rows, center deck. Like the schoolteacher he was, Robert told us to sit, clapped his hands, and called us to attention.

"Okay, gang, now that I've finally got you all in one little bunch, I've got a few instructions." He wiped a drop of sweat from the end of his nose. "We have one house, and we all have to live there. The gals will be on the top floor and the fellas on the bottom floor. There is no dining room so we'll have to eat in the living room and that, fellas, is the only room on the second floor you may enter! Get that straight! We'll have no messing around. I'm responsible for every little blossom in my care, each tender chee-ild," he leered villain-like, pretending to twist his non-existent moustache. "I don't want to have to close the season with a bunch of pregnant females on my hands. Okay?" he said, gesturing nonchalantly with one hand. "This summer we hope to make some money. This will not be a vacation in an island paradise. If that's what you expect, then you'd better yell for them to stop the ferry. You'll work hard, but if you are truly dedicated you'll love, love, love it! Remember, you were handpicked because you show promise. Not one of you is a star. Not yet!"

Melodramatically he placed his hand over his heart, his eyes searching. "I want nothing more than your hard and devoted work. That's the only payment I ask. I'm picking up the tab for food and giving you a place to rest your weary heads, so let's work together as a team and we'll all benefit from the profits—I in pecuniary matters, and you by experience. I tell you now that after four summers on Catalina Island I haven't made a cent. Not one red cent! I've been lucky to break even. But hope springs eternal! Yes, hope springs eternal," he said looking suddenly dazed and exhausted from his breathless exhortation.

He paused, then looked at Jerry, a tall college kid with a press camera in his lap. "Load up the camera, Jerry, and let's get some pictures—the lovely ladies first." Robert wanted something sexy, a line-up along the deck rail with the ocean in the background. He directed Willa, Loretta, Robin, Fern, and me to turn sideways, rest our hands at our waists, arch our backs, point our breasts skyward, and smile.

"That's it! Now, lift your skirts with your other hand. Good! Karen, just a little higher. Smile! Okay, Jerry, shoot!"

Robert ignored all the tourists pressing near. But I could not. I was so embarrassed I wanted to jump into the ocean. "Okay, girls let's see you again in profile—suck it in and arch those backs. Swell! Lick those lips and make them shine. Toss those gorgeous locks and give us your gayest smiles. Perfect! Got that, Jerry?" Satisfied, he turned to face his audience. "Ladies and gentlemen, here you see the lovely ladies of the Island Players—performing every night at the Patio Theatre. We'd love to see *you* in the audience!" He pointed at a surprised old lady who blushed and covered her mouth. Robert turned to the crowd, poking at faces with one finger, "And you and you and you!" He swung around at attention and clicked his heels, motioning for both the girls and boys to follow. "Come along, kiddies. I want pictures of the whole bunch! The whole fam-damn-ly."

After we had toured the ferry—taking pictures by the lifeboats, at the captain's wheel, and with lifesavers around our necks—Robert decided that he wanted the two best-looking young men, Dale and Jared, to pose with me. We were going to stage a little drama—the boys rescuing the girl at sea.

"Lift Karen like you're putting her into the lifeboat," he directed. I reddened as I felt myself being hoisted off the deck by two handsome young strangers. "Put your arms around their shoulders," Robert barked. "Good. Now, hug your heroes close. Remember you are grateful—they're rescuing you from Davy Jones' Locker. Whoops, lift your skirt and cross your legs, Karen. Let's see those gorgeous gams."

It seemed like everyone on board had gathered around. I blushed, crossed my legs, and reached for the hem of my skirt, positioning it at my knees. "Higher!" he shouted. I jerked my skirt higher, hoping I hadn't gone too far. "Perfect! Now smile."

My face burning, tears gathering in a tight lump at the base of my throat, I wanted down but forced a smile.

"I said 'smile.' I didn't say 'show your teeth.'" Robert rolled his eyes. Then, as if talking to a child he said, "If you expect to be an actress, honeybunch, you have to learn to smile on command. There's a definite art to turning on a sincere smile. Let your eyes smile too, not just your mouth." I made another attempt and felt a rush of tears. "Christ! Can't you smile?" Robert shouted.

"I'm sorry—the boat—my stomach's kind of upset," I lied.

Feeling that my life depended upon it, I put everything I had into a smile that I hoped would do. Evidently it did—or else Robert had given up. The picture was taken and the manly hunks lowered me to the deck.

I watched as the other girls posed for photographs. They seemed relaxed, like they were having fun. They felt at ease tossing their curls, enjoying the camera's eye on their bodies. *No shy little girl is going to get anywhere in this business,* I told myself.

Finally, Robert had all the pictures he wanted and we were excused. Willa grabbed me by the arm and quickly guided me through the crowd. We descended a metal staircase to a narrow passage just over the water and sat down on an empty bench. I took a deep breath of cool salty air as the hot sun warmed me. The water intensified to deep navy blue dotted with whitecaps. Hundreds of sea gulls circled the boat, diving and calling to us. In the distance, I could see the green sloping hills of Catalina Island rising above the white beach which ran ribbon-like above the blue water.

"Look! Flying fish." Willa pointed as the wind wrapped her long black hair around her face.

I leaned over the rail to watch them sail near the water's surface. "They look like fish with wings!"

"They are," Willa laughed. "Look! The beach-boys."

Dozens of boys—legs kicking a froth, arms splashing—swam toward the boat. Some had already reached its side and were so close that I wondered why the ferry didn't crush them. I could see coins tossed from the upper deck fall like silvery rain, over an ocean full of sprawling arms and legs. I threw the little change I had to a trio of brown bodies just below me. One boy caught a coin in mid-air and quickly inserted it into his bulging mouth.

"Do girls ever swim out?" I was thinking I'd like to try it.

"Not that I've seen."

The boys followed the boat to the dock, where they swam for the beach, scurrying everywhere, dropping on the warm sand to count their coins. *What a strange and exciting summer this is going to be,* I thought. A genuine smile must have lit my whole face.

* * *

We lived high on a hill overlooking Avalon, a little town built beside the half-round bay. The 1929 Catalina Casino at the water's edge was closed and shuttered. The town had seen better days. The island itself was mountainous and forested, with herds of buffalo and wild places that we would never see. Our days and nights would be spent working at the theatre.

The two-story wooden clapboard, badly in need of paint, had been built early in the twentieth century. The small yard off the front porch was overgrown with weeds, but a scattering of flowers from the garden's heyday had survived—red, white, and pink geraniums, a patch of white daisies in the overgrown lawn, and a broken trellis bent from the weight of hot pink bougainvillea. A lovely old fig tree stood high against the front of the house, its branches so close that we could sit on the couch in the sitting room, stick our hands out the open window, and pluck ripe figs to eat.

Except for the darkroom, where Jerry taught me how to develop black and white publicity photos, I never saw the first floor of the house. The upper rooms included a large sitting room, a small made-over kitchen, a tiny tower room with a view of the bay, and three bedrooms. Willa and I shared a small room with twin beds. Loretta and Fern shared another, and Lila, our housemother, cook, and elder character actress, bunked with Robin, the youngest member of the cast. At the very end of the upstairs hall a door opened directly into a shower stall through which you had to pass to get to the toilet and sink. It was the only bathroom in the house.

Robert announced that something *had* to be done about the number of "brownettes" in the troupe. Willa's hair was black and she would do as is. But Fern, Loretta, Robin, and I all had medium brown hair. Fern, our gamine, and Robin, our innocent girl-next-door, would be just fine with brown hair. As for long-legged elegant Loretta, she would be transformed into a redhead. "And we need a Marilyn," Robert said. "You're elected, Karen, you're gonna be our blonde sexpot." I protested, but Robert's mind was made up.

Robert footed the bill for the hair dye and peroxide and enlisted Lila to do the hairdressing. I took comfort from the fact that she bleached her own hair and probably knew what she was doing.

At the age of fifty-three Lila was just beginning her acting career. Robert probably paid her to be our housemother, cook, and seamstress. As an added inducement, she would also play all the mothers and grandmothers. Her sun-leathered face showed every minute of the twenty-three years of misery she had endured while married to the "no-good bum of a husband" she finally divorced.

During our hair-dyeing party in the kitchen, Lila applied a stinging, foul-smelling solution to my hair and set a timer. While my head cooked, she dyed Loretta's hair at the sink. Before long Loretta's long brown hair tumbled into luscious red curls and my hair glowed bright platinum.

*   *   *

We began our repertory season with rehearsals for our first play, *Camille, or Lady of the Camellias*, a melodrama starring Loretta as Camille and tall, dark, and handsome Dale as her lover. I don't remember who wrote the play, but the plot was taken from the Alexander Dumas story about a high-priced prostitute with consumption—the same story told in *La Traviata*. Under Robert's direction we played it for laughs. Loretta's Camille had a fake-sounding, way too persistent cough. Every one of her prolonged coughing spells produced gales of laughter from the audience.

I had two small parts: a barefoot peasant girl costumed in a low-cut bustier and peasant skirt and Gabrielle, one of Camille's rich girlfriends, who wore a décolleté-revealing pink ball gown. Both characters looked like Marilyn Monroe in period costume.

A week after we had arrived on the island we opened with *Camille* and performed the show every night while rehearsing *Fashion, or Life in New York,* a farce written in 1845 by Anna Cora Mowatt. In *Fashion* I played Seraphina Tiffany, a belle, daughter of a wealthy merchant and his fashion conscious wife. Robert had me play her with a whiney Brooklyn accent; every one of her gowns was split up the middle for a look at my gams. Once we had rehearsed *Fashion* for a week it was added to our repertoire and we began rehearsals on our third play, *Maria Marten, or Murder in the Old Stone*

Barn, a Gay Nineties melodrama. And so it went, until we had a different play or variety show every night of the week—all comedies for the pleasure of fun-loving summer crowds.

The Patio Theatre was a magical place with all kinds of interesting options for stage production. It wasn't a theatre at all, but an enclosed Spanish arcade with a bell tower, probably built in the twenties. At its center, the brick and tile piazza where we performed in the round was surrounded by a garden of aloes. When the script called for it, we used the bell tower—a good place for ghosts or suicidal maidens to appear. The broad stairs to the tower offered a dramatic setting for a sword fight or a triumphal procession, and the landing at the top could be used like a traditional stage. The garden paths made excellent exits and entrances or settings for outdoor scenes. The audience sat at the edge of the garden at small tables where the cast in full costume and makeup served sodas and popcorn before the show and at intermission. The theatre could seat about a hundred people—if we were lucky, a hundred dollars a night at the box office.

The arcade itself was locked up except for the dressing rooms and the rooms we used to store sets and costumes. Robert had acquired a huge collection (many from the Ice Follies): hats for men and women, feather boas, boxes filled with paste jewels, gloves, gowns, coats, tuxedos and suits, wigs, everything we needed to outfit the characters in every imaginable period. If something needed alteration or mending, Lila went to work. Neither Willa nor I told Robert that we could sew or we would have had extra duties. Willa and I loved playing in the wardrobe room, trying on costumes and hats, getting a load of ourselves in the tall freestanding mirror.

Early on, Robert decided which actors made the best couples on stage. He always cast mysterious Loretta opposite suave, darkly handsome Dale; Willa's fragile dark beauty with Bruce, a Tab Hunter look-alike; and me (his Marilyn) with handsome, muscular, yet boyish Jared.

Though he was an older man of twenty-seven, I liked Jared right away. He'd written a collection of wonderful songs, played guitar, and seemed good-natured. For our variety show we sang duets together and played opposite one another in *Maria Marten* and *Prince of Liars.*

Biggest laugh-getter of the evening was the comedy team of Kline and Vorbeck. Cast as two Cockney rustics of the old "vaudeville rube" school of make-up and exaggerated acting, Kline rated high with the audience as the dumb rustic Tim Bobbin who helps bring the villain to justice. His comic make-up, his caricature of rustic simplicity, all attest to Kline's artistry as an accomplished young actor. Karen Vorbeck, the Players' blonde S-bomb, covers her natural beauty and appeal under a true farcical characterization as Anne Marten, sister of the ill-fated Maria. Her shrewish, teasing farm girl proved that the lovely blonde does not need to depend on her physical beauty but has much talent as a comedienne.

Jared liked me too. Early on while posing for a group photo, he'd tugged me onto his lap for a snuggle. A pop tune on the radio had given him an excuse to pull me into his arms for a dance. One night we sat in the garden, looking at the moon, talking about our plans for the future. Perched on the garden steps, we could see the line of palm trees on the beach, the lights of the town, and the moon reflecting off the water. He described his life in Beverly Hills, where he attended a theatre school.

"My first love is music. I've been at it since I was a kid," he said, "but in this day and age if you want a career in musical comedy, you'd better be able to do it all."

"But you're a good actor."

"Sure! I can act, but I'm in trouble if you ask me to dance." We agreed that if we were serious about continuing in musical theatre we had better take dance classes.

We hadn't been under the stars very long when he pulled me close and kissed me for the first time. As our lips parted he took my head in both of his hands, cupping my face in a gesture of tenderness. I thought he was about to say something sweet like, "I think I could fall in love." But, in one forceful movement, he pushed my face down over his open fly, forcing my nose to collide with his erect penis.

"God damn you!" I cursed, pushing away. Horrified, I ran up the garden steps into the house.

Shaken, feeling destroyed, I could not fall asleep. Late into the night Willa tried to comfort me. "How could he do something like that? I barely know him!" Everything was ruined. I wanted to go home. "How am I going to face him tomorrow?"

"Look, Karen," she said, as if worldly wise, "you have nothing to be ashamed of. He should worry about facing you."

"I have to play opposite him in everything—do you think Robert would—"

"If you want to be an actress," Willa, said, her soft voice coming through the darkness like a gentle hand, "you are going to run into people like that now and then. He's nothing but a bully and like all bullies you'll have to stand up to him."

"How?" I hadn't a clue.

"You ignore him. If you report him to Robert, he'll get even worse. Just keep your distance, be alert to his movements, and let it pass."

The next day, when Jared ran into me in the hallway upstairs, he greeted me with a snarl, grabbed me roughly by the arm, and jerked me close enough to whisper, "I know what Karen likes to eat."

I understood the warning. If I told on him he would say that I had initiated the whole thing.

Hoping that his passion for humiliating me would subside, I had decided to take Willa's advice and ignore him. Off stage Jared couldn't look at me without sneering. On stage, as we played lovers, he thoroughly enjoyed watching me struggle with my fear and loathing.

* * *

Besides all-day rehearsals, we had a different performance every night, weekend matinees (one a children's show with scenes, songs, and dances for children), all night sessions studying our lines, and occasional night rehearsals after the show. In my spare time I made a little money on a photo shoot at some ruins in the mountains, where I modeled a gold *peau de soie* evening gown from a couturier's new collection. I don't remember his name. The designer's people drove me up into the hills to the ruins of a stone mansion. They dressed me behind a crumbling stone wall and posed me standing in high heels on a decaying staircase. Overlooking the island and the sea, I teetered at the edge of what felt like "land's end" and smiled for the camera. "Don't smile," the photographer said. They wanted my dark eyes and shiny lips to look seductive, yet dignified.

The Island Players had to meet the ferry every day. Carrying Robert's signs, we went in small committees of two or three. The guys wore tails and top hats and the girls matching Gay Nineties costumes (minus the skirts) with big bows bouncing over our rear ends, fish-net stockings, high heels, and plumed hats. We walked down the main street toward the landing wearing our bonnets and bows, past restaurants, bars, and shops on the waterfront. Local shop owners got used to seeing us prance by every day as they busied themselves for the onslaught of tourists. At the dock, we smiled at disembarking day-trippers, held up our signs, and looked pretty. We all hated meeting the ferry, but it wasn't so bad when I got to go with Willa. I liked being with Willa no matter what we had to do.

On our march to the dock, a handsome young cop said "Hi!" every time we passed his corner. One day we stopped to chat with Dan Manchester, a San Jose State College criminology student who had come to Catalina to work as a policeman for the summer. Eager to save money for school, he had taken a second job operating the diving bell tram. One day, he asked me to meet him that night after the show for a walk on the beach.

*　*　*

Dan, with the sweet smile and twinkle in his blue-green eyes, brought a bottle of white wine and two stemmed glasses. For my first taste of wine, we sat in the sand and rested our backs against a palm tree. I didn't like the dry sharpness of the wine and sipped slowly, lying about how much I liked it.

We said the things a boy and girl say when they are getting to know one another, but Dan learned more about me than I learned about him. He wasn't a talker. By the time the bottle was empty, I liked wine.

Usually when I had an hour free, I'd head for the beach with *The Prophet*, a little book my grandmother had given me, or the periodical *Science of Mind*. I had stumbled upon the first spasms of the New Age: self-discovery and the link between mind, body, and spirit with plenty of positive thinking thrown in. But on the day Dan asked me to meet him after he got off work, I'd brought nothing to read. He was going to dive for abalone off the point and had invited me to come along.

I saw him on the diving bell tram, naked from the waist up, almost black from the sun. He waved, and my heart flew around with butterflies. He jumped off the tram, grabbed his bag and headed my way, the best-looking young man I had ever seen off a movie screen.

"Hi, white nose," he said running his finger through the patch of zinc oxide on my peeling nose. Smiling warmly, he took my arm and guided me down the street toward the Casino. "Want to know the good news?"

"Of course!"

"Look at that cloudless sky and isn't that water unusually blue?" He looked so happy that I expected him to break into a skip. "And I don't have to work! Do you?"

"No, I don't!" I shouted.

As soon as the beach popped into view, Dan ran for the sand and unpacked his bag. He had masks and fins for of us, and an abalone iron. He put on his fins and ran like a duck toward the surf. I followed. Hitting the surf, he swam straight out past the breakers into deep water. When I reached the spot where he treaded water waiting for me, he motioned for me to follow and we swam toward a large outcropping of rocks about thirty yards out. The water was calmer there, and I had gotten used to its chill. Dan had climbed up on the little island to wait for me. He took my hand and pulled me out of the water. I brushed against him as I tried to get my footing, and he folded me into his arms and kissed me for the first time. He tasted like the sea and something deliciously Dan. When I stopped trembling inside, I had to say something to hide how I felt. "Our own private island." I couldn't say what I was thinking.

"I like that idea." He winked and squeezed my hand. He lowered his mask, slid off the rocks into the water, and disappeared.

Adjusting my mask, I eased myself down the rocks into the water, slowly submerging myself. I had never snorkeled in deep water before. Wrapped in quiet, I saw the kelp forest sway, waving blue, green, and gold ribbons in slow motion. From the depths of that languorous rhythm darted a bright school of shimmering orange fish.

I surfaced for air, filled my lungs, and pushed from the side of the rock. Swimming toward the bottom, I watched bubbles leave my nose and slowly rise to the surface. Yellow sand rose in clouds as my fins touched the ocean floor. I needed air and swam toward the light, scattering a school of silver mackerels.

Gasping, I broke through the water close to the spot where Dan had surfaced. He waved for me to follow and dove under. He'd found an abalone bed and as I watched used the iron to pry flat golden shells almost as big as his head from the rocks. He looked like he knew what he was doing.

That night at his apartment, Dan cooked for me. He pounded the abalone flat, rolled it in flour, and sautéed it in butter. "Me, Big Hunter—cooks for little woman."

As I made the salad I wondered how I could possibly resist him. He opened the wine and led me out to his little balcony overlooking the town and the bay. We sat on the rumpled old porch swing with our plates in our laps and watched the sun set.

Though we found out how passionate we were together, we stayed out of bed. I was determined to be a good girl, and he was man enough to control himself. Dan was a good cop, a superhero, but I already knew he wasn't the soul mate my mother said I should find.

*　*　*

The Island Players rehearsed from seven in the morning until dinner at five. We had two hours to rest before we went to the theatre at seven—curtain at eight. I'd learned accents: proper British, street Cockney, southern drawl, and Brooklyn. One night when I was supposed to be in Brooklyn, I lapsed into the back streets of London and knew that I was tired. I learned how to dance in the chorus for one of Willa's dance numbers. And I learned how to sword-fight for *Taming of the Shrew*, in which I played a young man in only one scene and got the rest of the night off to be with Dan.

Robert put together a variety show filled with songs, dances, and famous scenes from popular plays. One night during a scene Jared gave me a scurrilous look and fed me the wrong line, then watched with glee as I tried to squirm my way back into the scene.

I was Robert's glittering Marilyn in a gown of red sequins so tight I could hardly walk. He smothered me in faux diamonds and had me vamp my way down the long bell tower staircase singing *Diamonds Are a Girl's Best Friend*. Everyone said I looked and sounded just like Marilyn.

As part of our variety show Robert picked scenes from three hit plays: *Bus Stop*, *Anastasia*, and *My Fair Lady*. Both *Bus Stop* and *Anastasia* had been big movies in 1956, and *My Fair Lady* remained the biggest hit on Broadway. He gave me all the leading roles.

Every day Willa and I talked about our dream—being discovered by a Hollywood film producer or a Broadway director. Every night we hoped *he* was in the audience. We'd heard about Lana Turner, how she'd ditched school one day to hang out at a drugstore. A big Hollywood producer had seen her sitting at the soda fountain sipping an ice cream soda. "How'd you like to be a movie star?" he asked. The rest was history. And just a year or so before, film director Otto Preminger, in a hugely publicized search, had scoured small town America to find the perfect young girl to play Joan of Arc. He was going to film the movie version of Shaw's *Saint Joan* and wanted an unknown to star. In Iowa, he'd found seventeen-year-old Jean Seberg. We believed we could be discovered too—we just had to keep practicing our craft, be in the right place at the right time, and hope for some luck.

One day on my way to rehearsals, a man approached me on the street. He asked if I was a model. I told him I worked at the theatre. He gave me the once over, said he was a Hollywood photographer, and told me he thought I was pretty. He asked if I would come to his studio to pose for pictures. My heart pounded with excitement as I took his card. I told him I would show up that night about eleven-thirty, after the show.

Clutching his card in my hand, I headed to the theatre. Robert was busy, rehearsing a scene with Jared and Dale. The moment they took a break, I showed Robert the photographer's card and told him about my good luck. Robert took one look at the card and roared, "You are such a mark!"

"What's a mark?"

He rolled his eyes and shook his head. "That's the guy who bags groceries at the market," Robert said, shaking the business card in my face. "He's got a camera, all right, but no film."

"How do you know?" I asked, unable to hide my disappointment.

"He invites dumb broads like you up to his lair and seduces them."

Jared looked at me like I was an idiot, and they all laughed at how gullible I was.

"Stay away from that guy!" Robert commanded.

Dripping with diamonds, under a black-feathered hat and clinging red dress, I played Rosa in *Prince of Liars*. My love interest, Jared, played a drunkard. I had to kiss him every night on stage, where he made the most of his sincere looks of love and tender kisses. In one of our scenes, I had to cross downstage in front of him while he was seated in a chair. During rehearsal he put out his foot and tripped me. I took a painful fall, skinning my knee on the stone floor. No one saw what happened, but I knew. I got up off the floor, apologized for being clumsy and carried on. I nursed my bloodied knee, afraid to complain. But I cursed him every minute of the hour I had to spend re-weaving the hole in my stockings.

*   *   *

Dan and I laughed about how different we were. We joked about being the *actress* and the *cop*—the artist and the civil servant. He was an uncomplicated young man, good to the core, without a neurotic bone in his body. After work at night, we took long walks on the beach, holding hands and brushing shoulders, sometimes saying nothing. The moon's pull, the surf lapping the shore seemed eloquent enough.

One night from the top of the table, as I undulated Marilyn-style to *Old Black Magic,* I saw Dan standing in the dark at the back of the theatre leaning against the stucco wall in his police uniform, holding his hat in his hand. Seeing him there in the dark, knowing he was watching me, I sang the song on key just for him.

Very late that night after work and a walk on the beach, we followed the full moon up the hill to his apartment. Breaking the intense silence of the night, Dan whistled a low sweet song.

How beautiful, I thought, the bright surreal shadows cast on the houses and the deserted street. I looked at Dan, his head thrown back revealing the graceful curve of his throat as he whistled. His eyes fixed in the direction of the moon and our ascent, he looked beautiful to me. That night, as the bright Catalina moon and the salt breeze wafted in through his bedroom window, it was impossible for us to resist.

Dan and I had talked about school and my father's decision not to send me back. He told me about San Jose State College and its first-rate theatre department, suggesting that I try to get in there. Maybe my mother could afford a state college. I wrote my mother with this idea (leaving out the part about Dan), and she agreed. My transcripts were sent from CWC, and I was accepted at San Jose State. At the end of summer Dan and I would not have to part.

*   *   *

It was hard to say good-bye to Willa, the island, the old house on the hill, to our sturdy optimistic little troupe of actors and a summer of adventure and hard work. Our season of music, high camp, and melodrama had entertained lots of tourists, but we had hardly made a penny for Robert. He would return to his teaching job in September, but I doubt that Robert was disappointed. He enjoyed playing the part of a hard-nosed businessman, but we all knew that he did the whole thing for fun.

Before we left the island, Robert pulled me aside. He said that he would like to take me for auditions in Hollywood. I was an exceptional talent, he said, and he thought he might be able to help me break into the movies. I couldn't believe his generosity, that he wanted to give me my big break.

Sisters on the beach with their visiting father in Carpenteria, CA, 1955 (L-R
Karen, Susan, Miles, Gretchen)

Karen modeling Miss Atomic
Energy crown, 1955

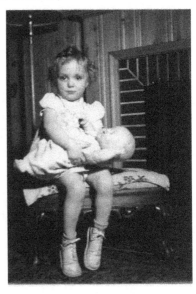

Karen with Tommy doll with
open and shut eyes, 1941

Karen and Jim on their wedding
day, 1959

Bette in Shady Lane garden, 1956

Colorado Women's College, 1957

Susan, Gretchen, Karen, and
Bette, 1955

16

Hollywood

1957

After my screen test, the director clapped his hands gleefully and yelled:
"She can't talk! She can't act! She's sensational!" —Ava Gardner

WE WERE TO meet Robert at his college and drive together to
Twentieth Century Fox.

Because freeway driving terrified my mother, I took the wheel
for the drive to L.A., braving the traffic as Mother clenched her teeth
and gripped the door brace. Sometimes when a car entered on the
right from an on-ramp or I sped up to pass, she would yelp and
throw her feet up on the dashboard, bracing herself for a crash.

We met Robert, and on the drive I imagined that once inside the
studio gate I would see Marilyn and Mitzi standing on a street
corner talking to Shirley Jones. I thought I'd see bit players in
makeup and costume rushing from set to set—or at least one wild
bohemian director. But we walked alone through empty streets to
the new talent office, entering a stylishly decorated room where
three secretaries sat at three important-looking desks.

Robert gave his name, and we were shown into a still larger room where a big man sat behind a big desk looking very powerful. Introductions followed, and the three of us sat down like automatons controlled by a button on his desk.

I felt miniscule.

Mr. B welcomed us with a resounding voice, as if he were speaking to the last row of a thousand-seat theatre. I shrunk as he looked hard at me and boomed, "How much do you weigh?"

"A hundred-twenty-uh—five," I answered, feeling myself puff up, fat as a startled toad.

He shook his head sadly and whispered to himself. "Too much. Too, too much."

All of a sudden Mr. B wanted to tell me about talented girls who never got anywhere in show business because they had fat hips, rotund legs, or manly arms. "My dear," he bellowed, "in your present condition all you could play is second-lead."

"Oh, that's all right," I croaked, shaking inside with shame. "I don't have to play the lead."

"My dear, one's physical appearance is everything in film. We can always use camera tricks to make you girls look like you can act."

With every fiber of my being I disagreed but said nothing.

My mother paled, and Robert looked nervous. I had never seen bombastic Robert when he wasn't in command, but across Mr. B's desk he seemed downright reverential.

"Gloria!" he called. Gloria appeared with a steno pad in hand. "Take dictation: Saw Karen Vorbeck today," he mentioned the date. "Has experience in summer stock with Robert Larson. Told her to lose weight. She promised to do same, and send me a photo when she has. That'll do, Gloria." He turned to me and said, with all sincerity, "I hope you'll do something about your problem, young lady."

Then mercifully directing his attention away from me, he spoke to Robert. "I know how talented she must be or you wouldn't vouch for her."

With thank yous all around, we shook hands and raced for the door. His parting words? "Lose fifteen pounds and next time you are in a show let me know. I'll come see you."

We all lit cigarettes and, puffing thoughtfully, walked silently to the car. But on the drive to MGM, Robert had to talk. "I'm sorry, Karen. I should have warned you that these movie folks are blunt. At this level of the business, you know, it's dog-eat-dog. But don't be discouraged."

MGM looked even larger and more impressive than Twentieth Century Fox, and to my delight, the streets bustled with show people. In vain I searched passing faces for a glimpse of Debbie Reynolds or Gene Kelly. We found the new talent office, went in, and waited almost half an hour. I thought I was prepared for anything.

Finally, Mr. T's secretary brought us into the office of a tall, handsome man about forty-five. He greeted us so warmly that I felt at ease. Once we had settled in our chairs he opened with a question.

"How much do you weigh, young lady?"

"A hundred—uh—fifteen," I mumbled, as my stomach hopped on the elevator.

Without comment he wrote my answer on a notepad. He seemed to know Robert well and asked him questions about my experience. With more than enough superlatives, Robert mentioned the high points of my performances on Catalina Island. Then they lapsed into talk about old times, laughing and telling stories about old friends. Robert tried to put in a plug for me from time to time.

"You see, Karen," Mr. T said during a pause in their chatter, "in the movies we can make anyone *look* like they can act. Robert says you're good, but we are looking for another Marilyn or a Lana. You just aren't pretty enough." Then he shot Robert a look: *you should know better than waste my time.* Before we left, Mr. T smiled very warmly, shook my hand, and said, "Karen, nice meeting you. I'm sure you'll lose all that baby fat someday."

It was over. I had blown my big break. Worse, I had been put under a microscope, dissected, and left to bleed to death in front of my mother. On our way to the parking lot we whipped out our cigarettes as Robert burbled apologies for both men's blunt disregard for my feelings.

"It's not your fault—film adds ten pounds—any fool can see how pretty you are. How hard is it to lose the weight, anyway—they ought to know you'd lose the goddamn weight! It's a bitch trying to break into this business—excuse my French, Mrs. Vorbeck."

"That's okay," Mother moaned.

"You are one of the most talented girls I've ever seen, and if you don't make it—there's no justice in this goddamn world. Sorry, there's my French again, Mrs. Vorbeck."

We couldn't even take comfort in the fact that Julie Andrews would not be pretty enough to play Liza Doolittle in the movie version of *My Fair Lady*. That hadn't happened yet. We didn't know that someday Barbra Streisand and her exotic nose would play romantic leads.

We headed for Paramount studios, where Robert had arranged for us to meet up with a friend for dinner. As we entered the studio gates I saw Cornell Wilde standing on the corner talking to two men. I'd rather have seen William Holden or Gary Cooper. At last I knew for certain that I would never get to work in a film with anyone like even Cornell Wilde.

While the three of us waited, silently, desolately in his friend's office, Robert suddenly jerked to attention.

"Dammit! I've got an idea!" He stood up and spoke to the secretary. "Who's the new talent director here?"

With the name and phone number in hand he picked up the phone.

"No! No, please!" I pleaded, "Let's not bother him."

Robert ignored me and dialed. "Hello, Milton!" he oozed into the phone. "This is Robert Larson. I doubt if you'll remember me."

I doubted it too.

"Look, Milton, I'm here to see Bob Greene and I've got this pretty blonde with me. I know you'll never forgive me if I don't bring her by." Evidently Milton agreed, because we immediately headed for the new talent office, where we entered a small humble room with a few empty chairs waiting against the walls. Robert seemed stumped. He looked down a hallway and yelled, "Milton?" Milton stuck his head out of a door and motioned for us to come.

The new talent director did not waste an ounce of charm on us. We made introductions—nervous me, nervous Robert, nervous Mother. He wanted to know which plays I'd done and what I did best.

"Would you do a scene for me?"

I said I would.

"Let's do an audition for a screen test," he said, rummaging around in a bookcase full of scripts. "What did you do last?"

"She was wonderful in *Bus Stop*," Robert suggested, describing the scene I'd done with Jared on Catalina Island.

"Good," he said, finding scripts. He offered one to me and the other to Robert. "Read with her." He ushered us into a soundproof room with a big window and microphones.

Mr. Lewis, his secretary, and my mother sat in a room on the other side of the glass, in what looked like theatre seats. When he gave a signal for us to begin I put down the script and did the scene from memory. It felt good. I could tell I was good.

When it was over, I looked through the glass and Milton was smiling. My mother looked thrilled. Even the secretary's face held a look of lingering pleasure.

When Robert and I returned to the seating area, Milton smiled a lot and said, "You are a definite talent." Then to his secretary, "Get some information on this gal."

After I had answered all her questions, Milton got up to leave. He thanked us for coming in to see him and left the room.

"We'll call you," he hollered down the hall.

Robert said that meant I'd never hear from him.

* * *

In those days, I had a talent for burying my hurts so deep that I could not find them. Instead of feeling low or sad, I wrote a story about my adventure at the three major studios. Pushing away the pain, I turned the whole thing into a self-deprecating joke. One day my hurt would surface, but it would appear so altered and mixed up with all the other feelings I never allowed myself to feel that I would have no idea what hit me.

I packed my bags for college and put my hopes on a stage career. *So what if I'm not pretty enough for Hollywood. I'll go to New York.*

17

Not Pretty Enough

1957

"I never thought I'd land in pictures with a face like mine." —Audrey Hepburn

MY MOTHER HELPED me settle into Lee Ann Hall, a massive old Victorian house a few blocks from the college. Old houses were used as temporary dorms because of overcrowding. Lee Ann Hall was almost as shabby as our house on the hill at Catalina but held none of its charm. Downstairs a pay phone hung on the wall across from a common room furnished with dog-eared couches where the stench of cigarette smoke settled over a portable TV, usually tuned to a soap opera.

San Jose and the college looked huge to me, the girl from a small town in the mountains. The first thing I did was call Dan. I felt better knowing he was there, but the minute I saw him I knew everything had changed. He was out of context. I didn't feel the same about him or myself away from Catalina Island. I had no confidence. I didn't know why or what made me so afraid. Not of him, but of something lying in wait for me.

Maybe it's because I'm new, I counseled myself, trying to remember how it felt when I first went to Ojai. *I'll adjust.*

I compared myself to his buddies' girlfriends: pretty girls, too purposeful in their friendliness toward handsome Dan's new girlfriend. I thought they would never have befriended me if I wasn't his girl. Two of the girlfriends wore sparkling diamond engagement rings. They liked drinking beer with the boys—and football—they even understood the game. They wanted to join sororities and get married, but most appallingly they were having the time of their lives.

Compared to little CWC with its park-like campus dotted with English-style manor houses, San Jose State looked like a polished granite city. Some classes were held in amphitheaters so large that the teacher had to use a microphone. The buildings loomed over and around me and my newest dirty little secret. *I'm not pretty enough.* The new talent director at MGM had told me so.

If only I were pretty enough the director would place me in front of the cameras, like just the perfect vase placed on a table by a skillful set decorator. He would tell me how to move, coax tears from my eyes, or tickle a laugh from my belly. He would make it look like I could act. The cameraman would frame the picture to perfectly tell the story. The film editor would throw every false move into the wastebasket. After all, moving pictures are more like paintings than like plays. The paint has no talent; the man with the brush has the skill.

* * *

Most of the girls at Lee Ann Hall wanted to be teachers until they got married. They wanted to move out of the dump where we lived and into one of the sorority mansions. I knew nothing about sororities, except that my grandmother had been a Tri Delt when she attended Knox College. She'd said it would thrill her to pieces if I became a Tri Delt too. When I told the girls, they said I couldn't just expect to join the sorority of my choice. I had to be chosen. Some of the sororities, they said, were more desirable because their girls were beautiful and popular and smart.

Not long after school began, we Lee Ann Hall girls dressed in our prettiest afternoon dresses, high-heeled shoes, and gloves to make the round of sorority teas. We would introduce ourselves at each tea, make a favorable impression, leave our calling cards and hope that one of the sororities liked us enough to ask us to join. Luckily my grandmother had made sure that I had calling cards with my name engraved in Edwardian script.

I entered the Tri Delt mansion through elegantly paneled front doors opening into a long hall with a grand staircase. Three smiling, very well-dressed young women sat at a table near the entrance taking names and calling cards. Maybe their job was sorting cards into little piles: beautiful, intelligent, dumb, and ugly.

I looked into the front parlor and heaved a sigh of relief. A large table in front of the fireplace was set with a lace tablecloth, silver tea service, and trays full of dainty-looking sandwiches and sweets. Stricken by nervous hunger, I removed my gloves, slipped them into my purse, and headed straight to the tea table. Everything looked delicious.

A sorority girl lurking near the petit fours asked me a friendly question. I answered with a smile, daintily nibbling a little sandwich. I knew how to be friendly even when I didn't want to. Suddenly I hated my dress, my shoes pinched, and I felt like that toad in Mr. T's office. Ravenous, I grabbed a petit four and popped the whole thing into my mouth, then licked my thumb and forefinger as I smiled and winked at the sorority girl. She smiled. I was glad when she turned to glance across the room, giving me a chance to cram a finger sandwich on pink bread into my mouth.

She excused herself. I watched her walk toward a gathering of eager young women, girdled hips wrenching primly under her straight skirt. I tried to picture myself as her sorority sister, her bosom buddy, having breakfast in our pajamas around the table in the kitchen. But I couldn't concentrate. A distracting question kept popping into my head. *Where did they find pink bread?*

By the time I walked through the second mansion door and found another grand staircase and another lace-covered table with silver tea service and tiny sweet and savory morsels to eat, I didn't want to join a sorority. I thought I loathed those fervent young women in polka dot dresses and pastel suits. I thought I didn't belong in those stuffy rooms with all those young ladies who would grow old playing bridge and gossiping. Just like my Mother, I was above all that. But perhaps I was afraid they wouldn't choose me. Had I decided to reject them first?

I excused myself, walked back to Lee Ann Hall, and hung my afternoon party dress in the closet. In case anybody asked why I didn't want to be in a sorority, I had a little speech ready.

"I want to act on stage," I would say. "Not in my life."

* * *

In the drama department everyone, except me, spoke beautiful stage English. I could speak like that on stage, but I couldn't attach myself to girls my age who sounded like Joan Fontaine as they ordered bad coffee and a hot dog in the campus snack bar. My prospects for getting a part in a play seemed nonexistent to me. I believed I would have to attend classes for at least a year before I'd be cast in a major production. Maybe that was a rule.

I felt even worse after seeing a play in the main theatre—a Greek tragedy with flowing costumes and long, serious speeches. The lighting was dramatically gloomy, the whole production dark. A student leading lady threw herself to the stage floor and, in words I barely understood, cried out in anguish. I tried to picture myself on that big stage. I knew that I could never prostrate myself like that, or understand a role that deep, or make that sound. Nothing in my life had prepared me to make that sound.

What tragedy I had experienced by the time I was nineteen I'd been afraid to feel. I brushed it off or did not defend myself and had hidden it away in a *Don't Think About That Anymore* trunk. The trunk existed in my nightmares, hidden in a shadowy attic near a rolled-up rug. I dreamed I'd killed someone and left the body to molder in that rug. Throughout the nightmare someone was always coming to search the attic, unroll the rug, and discover the body and my crime.

I had spent the summer doing comedy, melodrama, and borderline slap-stick. That's what I was good at. I was in the wrong place. But worse, I was the wrong person. I didn't want to be a comedienne, I wanted to be a great dramatic actress—but I couldn't. I wasn't good enough—smart enough—pretty enough.

My classes in acting and voice and the required liberal arts courses did not go well. I didn't study. History and English didn't interest me. In acting class the teachers seemed to look right through me, favoring with smiles and friendly asides the young actors they had known from the year before. I was the only Marilyn Monroe in a room full of Kathrine Hepburns. More fiercely than ever, I wanted to be someone else—to walk on stage and mercifully become a different person.

For my first monologue, I selected the farewell scene from *Our Town*. My teacher wrote a critique and, like almost everything else, I saved it in my scrapbook:

> More emphasis in placing vowels forward. Communication was good, wistful and touching. Emotion shown well in voice. Did not place tone on the wall. You must project. Pounced on words, tone wasn't consistently sustained, lost control of diaphragm. Suffered from lack of preparation. You seemed a little tired and unsure of yourself. You shook—do relaxing exercises before you recite. Better come to me for help.

I never went for help. After classes, I returned to Lee Ann Hall and with other stupefied young women wasted hours in the sitting room smoking, watching soap operas, and eating junk food as I waited for it to get dark, for Dan to pick me up, for him to make love to me.

Sometimes, after Dan finally arrived, he took me to movies, football games, and pep rallies. He couldn't understand why I didn't want to join a sorority and when I tried to explain, I sounded like a snob. I didn't tell him that I hated San Jose State or that I knew I would never fit in. There was no way I could tell Dan about that or the dead person inside me.

* * *

One night as I lay fully dressed beside him in his bed, I felt myself slip away.

"Why?" he asked, kissing me. "Why's my baby so sad?" He looked sad himself. But his melancholy seemed to reach me from far away, like something thin and wispy coming toward me through a wall. I wanted so badly to cheer myself up for him. But my mind had locked down and I could not speak.

"Don't kid me like this." There was an impatient edge to his voice.

I wanted to tell him I wasn't kidding, but I could not move my lips, to utter the words.

"Karen," he said, looking worried, "you've got to say something. You're scaring me." He looked so frightened that I began to cry. "What's the matter? Honey, please—what's the matter?"

Unable to answer his worried questions, I lay there stiff as a corpse, crying and trembling. My head felt as if it would explode. Though he held me through the night, I could not stop crying. Finally, I ran out of tears, and at dawn he drove me back to Lee Ann Hall, where I called my mother and asked her to come and get me.

*   *   *

I dyed my hair brown, got a job selling accessories at J. C. Penney in Ventura, and showed up for auditions at the Ojai Art Center, where Roger Clark was casting *Maid to Order*, a new play by Alfred L. Golden. I didn't know who Roger was then, but a story in the *Ojai Valley News* said that he had just finished a starring role in a soon-to-be-released film with Jeffrey Hunter. As a young man he'd made pictures with Marlene Dietrich and Joan Crawford; in 1951 he'd produced *Gramercy Ghost* starring June Lockhart on Broadway.

Maid to Order was a comedy in which mistaken identity and plot twists revolved around a young husband's fears that his sudden marriage to a woman his parents had never met would lead to disaster. I went home from the audition with the ingénue lead—a bride who shows up at her in-laws' front door at the same time they expect the new maid. For reasons I can no longer remember, she accepts the role as maid, which leads to lots of fun and nonsense.

Every day I put on a dress and drove to Ventura to work, helping women shoppers find the perfect handbags and accessories.

We searched for the right colors. I listened to and sympathized with their complaints about how many compartments or zippers were missing. Working all day in four-inch heels, I straightened packages of stockings, sorted belts back to the right hangers, and re-folded dozens of scarves. Every day my middle-aged boss tried to fondle me in the stock room.

Sandy and Anne were both away at college. I knew they were doing well and that made my failure even more shameful. But the thought of going back to school literally gave me nightmares.

I hadn't told my mother the truth, why I'd left school. When she asked, I did my best to look light-hearted while trashing the idea of studying history or anything else that kept me from getting on with my career.

I missed Dan and felt guilty for leaving so suddenly; I had literally fled. Soon after I came home, I called to apologize. "I didn't feel right having my mother and sisters sacrifice so that I could attend school." It was the only excuse I could come up with to make me sound worthy of his understanding and forgiveness, but it was not the truth.

He was cool on the phone. Right away, in so many words, he let me know that he didn't have time for a crazy lady. Our conversation was short, and after I hung up I told myself that he didn't mean that much to me anyway—it had just been a summer romance. I tried not to think about our conversation and stuffed it into the bulging trunk full of things I didn't want to remember: my guilt, my inability to be honest and real with him, the possibility that I was insane.

I still have nightmares about San Jose State.

* * *

Longing for the girl I'd been on Catalina Island, I began writing about my experiences in summer stock. It would be a book about a girl named Sandra Waggoner, the daughter of a wealthy doctor. I wrote about eight thousand words before I got stuck and quit. It wasn't long before I began again, this time changing the character's name to Catherine. I guess I thought that if I changed the name the writing would go better.

In my story I gave the young actress an involved and caring father who "spread his long arms wide to welcome his daughter." He knew his child's dreams. He hadn't been surprised that she had joined the stock company but so cherished his memory of her childhood that it made it hard for him to let her grow up. The girl in my story loved her father more than anyone. She treasured the way he made her feel safe and loved, just like he had when she was a child. When she says goodbye to her father at the airport he tells her how much he will miss her. He calls her "Kitten" and says how great she'll be on stage. He'll write every week and travel all the way from the Midwest to see her perform. He says he knows she'll deserve a standing ovation at the end of every show.

As I wrote the story I saw no irony in the father I had created. My own father never saw me on stage. As far as I could tell, he had no sentimental attachment to my childhood and no angst about my growing up. He never spoke of his pride in me. When he greeted me at the airport, he woodenly placed his hands at my waist to keep my exuberance at bay.

As I wrote the story about the young woman with the adoring father I made up a new reality, but I could never get her into bed with the cop, or make summer end, or take her off the island. I couldn't finish the story.

I wrote my father regularly. Most of my letters were cheerful, optimistic, and full of news. Sometimes I tried to write about feelings, but I was more starry-eyed than honest.

Typical letters from my father told of Grand Junction's weather and how many baseball games and plays he and Bonnie had seen or details about their vacations in Mexico or New Orleans. Sometimes he'd send along a favorite joke. But my father never asked questions about my life, sent encouraging words, or responded to the heart-rending love I sent in my letters.

*   *   *

Susan, Gretchen, and I went home for Christmas. Our father did not want to pay for three airline tickets, so we took the bus. We slept sitting up for two days, hobnobbed with everyone but the chickens and the goats, and ate our meals at bus stops. We considered it a big adventure. By the time we arrived we needed baths, clean clothes, and beds.

The big excitement at home was the new baby. With the luck of Henry VIII, my father had sired another daughter. The baby was only three months old, and we took turns giving her a bottle. While I was prepared to love my new sister, I wondered why such old people found it necessary to have a baby, all while feeling the sting of Daddy's adoration for his infant daughter.

18

Lost and Found

1958

"People often become actresses because of something they dislike about themselves: They pretend they are someone else." —Bette Davis

AFTER CHRISTMAS, WE went into rehearsal for *Maid to Order*. The play was set to open in late February. Patient, gentle, dignified Roger was nothing like bombastic Robert. Knowing so little about him except what I'd read in the newspaper, I went to rehearsals eager to learn.

Between 1936 and 1952, Alfred Golden, the playwright, had written four plays that opened on Broadway. As far as I am able to tell they were all comedies and had short runs. Roger had produced one of them. Golden had never had a big hit. He came to a number of our rehearsals and made some minor changes in the script, but I have no memory of him.

The rest of the cast of characters consisted of a middle-aged married couple, their caustically funny maid who gave them good reason to fire her, a handsome son, and his wife Nancy, who was comically mistaken as the new maid. I was Nancy.

While we were still in rehearsal, Roger invited me to lunch at his home in the country. The day was sunny and cloudless as I drove past orange groves to a neighborhood where expensive houses hid on hills at the top of long driveways. Roger welcomed me at the front door and led me through the foyer toward an expansive light-filled living room where a wall of glass doors opened onto a garden and pool.

Mrs. Clark, a small woman about his age, with luminous white skin and black hair, was waiting for us at a patio table under a white umbrella. She held a pitcher full of iced tea sprigged with mint. I'd met her before at the theatre and had found her charming. She asked me to sit down. Roger sat too. I watched as her manicured fingers packed tall glasses full of ice. She poured the tea and served shrimp and avocado salads, chatting about the garden and the years they'd been in the house. We spoke for a while about rehearsals—how things were going. I wondered why I had I been invited.

"Karen, all you need now is an agent in Hollywood," Roger said, answering my unasked question.

An agent? The thought startled me. My old enemy confusion kept me from thinking straight, from being genuine. I was terrified of Hollywood and couldn't remember why. It took only a second to right myself, to pull out of my free fall and land back at the patio table, sipping iced tea under a white umbrella. I lifted my chin hoping that would make me look older. I lit a cigarette and, inhaling deeply, composed myself.

"I'm surprised . . ." I said, the fingers of one hand brushing against my hair, my heart racing with excitement. *He thinks I'm good.* I crossed my legs at the ankles, pulling my feet to the side at a graceful angle—like I'd been taught by Miss Livingston at CWC. I hoped I looked like a movie star thinking over an important career move. "I'm surprised that you think I'm ready," I said, hoping that was the right thing to say.

"Yes, why not? You are very good! With a little hard work you can go as far as you want in this business." Then his kind eyes narrowed, his look intensified as he took me in. "Why don't you believe that? If *you* don't believe it no one else will."

He was disappointed by my lack of confidence, and I knew I'd handled it badly.

"You are overwhelming her, dear," Mrs. Clark said gently. "Give her a minute to digest what you've said."

I looked at him, a handsome older man about my father's age, and pushed away a guilty urge to climb onto his lap and be his little girl. To curl up in his arms, snuggle my face against his neck, and let him rock me.

"Being an actress," I said, "that's what I want more than anything else in the world."

"It's a hard life," Roger said, leaning back in his chair. As something inside him withdrew, he picked up the last of his iced tea and downed it. "Show biz is tough."

"We know lots of movie folks," Mrs. Clark said, "That's been our life. You'd be surprised by how unhappy many of them are." She shook her head pitiably as she refreshed her husband's drink. "Some are impossible egotists—not at all nice."

While I looked up to the Clarks and knew Mrs. Clark must know what she was talking about, I didn't believe her and half expected her husband to contradict her. But he remained silent, withdrawn, as she told me about the movie stars' skin troubles, how the makeup actors have to wear ruins their skin.

"Why, I know all kinds of stars," she said, her flawless white skin gleaming in the shade of the umbrella, "who wouldn't dare let anyone see them without makeup. After years of caking it on, their skin has turned sour. They look beautiful on screen, but you'd be shocked to see how bad they look in person!"

Her argument fell on deaf ears. Ruined skin seemed a small price to pay for a career in the movies.

"You know," I said, finally remembering. "I had interviews at Paramount, MGM, and Twentieth Century Fox, and all three new talent directors said I wasn't pretty enough for the movies."

The Clarks looked at me blankly. By then I'd lost the fifteen ugly pounds. "Of course you're pretty enough!" Roger barked. "What nonsense!"

"Besides, they can do all kinds of things to make people look better on film," Mrs. Clark said. "Elizabeth has—Taylor—" she said for my benefit. "Elizabeth has short legs, doesn't she, Roger." Roger nodded. "They let wardrobe work on problems like that and film around people's physical flaws."

"You're built a lot like Elizabeth," Roger said.

* * *

On opening night, the whole cast was nervous because we had big shots in the audience: George Gobel's manager, a movie producer, and Hollywood agent Mitchell Gertz. The show went well and my reviews were good.

> Karen Vorbeck again gives promise of a bright professional future, her talent not in the least diminished by her exceptional attractiveness.

By the time the curtain rang down on our last performance, I was dating several young men. I'll call them Tom, Dick, and Harry. By all counts I'd just been a big success in a play, but that did not take away my fears and the unnamed longing that followed me. Starved for love and in search of oblivion, I stepped out of the good girl role I'd played since I left Grand Junction.

On a Friday night I dallied over a candlelit supper and wine with Tom. Under the stars on Saturday night I danced with Dick to the music of the car radio. On Sunday night Harry drove to the beach, where we watched a full moon set over the water. I barely remember those young men whose arms I clung to as if it was love. In the back seats of cars parked at the beach or on lonely roads, in strange beds in strange houses, they did their best to make me feel better.

We hadn't had the sexual revolution yet. I was ahead of my time, with no idea that the revolution was coming. I wasn't a liberated woman, just the "little whore" Reggie said I was. I was taking risks. The only birth control available was condoms and the rhythm method—keeping track of your cycle on the calendar. I thought I was safe just before or just after my period. We didn't worry about STDs and there was no such thing as AIDS.

John Turner, the boy I'd dated my senior year, called for a date. Johnny was the boy who, after dates with me, knocked on another girl's door for sex so that I could be a nice girl. I hadn't seen Johnny since I'd gone away to college.

That night after burgers and a movie, Johnny didn't park his car in the driveway on Shady Lane like he used to. He drove out to the country and parked on a deserted road. We talked and kissed for a while, like we had in high school, but something about us was different. He'd changed his mind about my status as a nice girl, I guess, and touched me accordingly. We carried on for a while, in tune with one another, I thought, when he pulled away.

"I can't do this with you." His moonlit face had twisted into an ugly grimace, and he put both hands on the steering wheel. Shivering with disgust he said, "You're different. What's happened to you?"

"I'm a big girl now," I said, trying for a joke, hoping to turn my humiliation into something I could bear.

He shook his head sadly and turned the ignition key. He was taking me home because he couldn't stand to be near me. As he backed out of the dark lonely lane, I crawled across the wide front seat. Shuddering inside, I pressed against the cold steel door and came upon myself in a dark, terrifying time warp. Where was I, in another car moving ghost-like down another dark road beside another angry male? There was no mercy for me anywhere inside that car, not in my heart or his.

I got out of his car in the driveway on Shady Lane and went inside without saying goodbye. Everyone was asleep. I went into the kitchen and opened the refrigerator door looking for something. I stood there a moment staring at a plate full of leftover salad. I wasn't hungry. Slipping quietly into the bedroom I shared with Susan, I fished around under my pillow for my nightgown and went into the bathroom to undress.

I flipped on the light and looked in the mirror, where a pretty face startled me—brown hair, sun-streaked with gold, perfectly plucked and arched eyebrows, full, just-kissed-lips with traces of coral lipstick still brightening them. I looked into the dark, sad eyes. As tears spilled and raced down my cheeks, I wondered who stared back at me. All I knew was that I'd hated her forever.

Opening the medicine cabinet, I found the razor, removed the blade, and held it up to my face. Considering the mechanics of cutting my flesh, I stared at the curve of my throat and the sharp blade. I was too afraid.

*   *   *

After *Maid to Order* closed I didn't know what to do with myself. I quit my sales job and enrolled at Ventura College, where I took mostly art classes and made a little money modeling for life drawing classes.

One day before auditions had been publicized for the Art Center's next production, *Affairs of State* by French playwright Louis Verneuil, the phone rang. It was the director, Fiona Leeds. We had worked together before.

"We're casting *Affairs of State*," she said in her native English accent. "Do you know the play?"

"No, I'm sorry I don't."

"It doesn't matter. I'd like you to play Irene—the female lead. I've admired everything you've done for us at the Art Center." Her aristocratic accent made it sound like she couldn't be wrong. "The moment I finished reading the play I knew you'd be perfect!" she added. "Rehearsals begin in March."

Fiona had come to the states as a young woman during the twenties. By 1958 she was in her mid-fifties and looked like Margaret Rutherford—exactly like an English maiden lady should—especially in her roles as a published author and owner of The Little Book Shop in the arcade. Among the works she'd published were historical novels, a juvenile book, some romances, and two biographies—one on her friend Pauline Frederick, the great silent film star. In 1956 the Art Center had produced her romantic drama, the world premiere of *Take My Hand?* I didn't know how experienced she was as a director, but Fiona was exceedingly kind to me, helping me as I worked hard to play Irene, a role written for an actress approaching her thirties, not her twenties.

Irene Elliot, my character, was the plain niece of a retired but still influential senator. Celeste Holm played her on Broadway. For the role, I wore my hair parted on one side, flattened on top and held in place with a barrette, an unflattering style for me. Dark horn-rimmed glasses, a shapeless business suit, and flat shoes completed my transformation.

*   *   *

In April Pat Boone was singing *April Love* on the radio and I met Jim Ragsdale. During breaks between classes, I hung out in the coffee shop with friends, smoking, sipping cokes, and playing long impassioned games of hearts. Walt, one of my card-playing friends, worked on the college literary magazine with Jim, and they were good friends. One day, Jim stopped to watch us play. I can still see him resting his arms on the back of the booth, leaning his chin on his hands for a look at Walt's hand.

"Hey, man," Walt said. "Do you know everybody at this table?"

With greatly exaggerated, dreamy brown eye movements, Jim looked carefully at all his friends. "Everybody but her." He was pointing at me.

They all laughed. Walt, and some of the others, knew that ever since Jim had seen me in psychology class he had wanted to meet me.

On our first date, we went to the beach with three other couples, broke out the beer, built a bonfire in the sand, and roasted weenies and marshmallows as the sun set over the pink sea. One of the boys had a guitar, and we sang songs like *Goodnight Irene* and *So Long, It's Been Good to Know You*. When the tide came in and doused our fire, we pulled our blankets higher on the beach, staying late to talk—a bunch of smarty-pants college kids with ideas on how to change the world.

I liked Jim. He seemed more serious, more complex perhaps, than any young man I had ever dated. I thought he was handsome with his crew cut and soulful brown eyes. His broad shoulders and chest narrowed to a small waist and hips, just like Superman's. His perfect classical Greek nose led to a high forehead lined with curiously deep creases. He drove a beat-up old Ford sedan, tan with patches of gray primer coat, the upholstery so ragged that he covered it with a beach towel. He called her "Ole Bessy." She got him where he wanted to go—most of the time. But mostly I was intrigued by the fact that we had gone out for nearly three weeks and he had never kissed me. We had long, interesting conversations and I thought he liked me, but I was more than a little puzzled.

One afternoon after school, I left my mother's car in the parking lot and climbed into Ole Bessy for a drive with Jim to the beach. We watched the sun drop toward the sea as the waves gently spilled shiny water stains in the sand. He was quiet for a change, and I sat close to him. It didn't take much to put myself within kissing distance. I just leaned in, put my mouth within reach, and hoped.

I thought his kiss was too uncommitted, and it bothered me that his eyes never connected with mine. Afterwards, when I daydreamed about that kiss—and the two or three that followed—I decided that practice makes perfect.

* * *

On opening night, as I waited nervously off stage for my first entrance, I felt ready to play Irene. I'd fallen in love with the character, a plain young woman with confidence in herself, a fine education, and absolutely no interest in anything small minded, just her teaching career and the world of books. Just like my mother, minus the confidence and the career.

In the play Irene's Uncle Phillip, a former senator, is married to Constance, a beautiful woman thirty years his junior. But Constance wants a divorce, citing the difference in their ages and her desire to "live more intensely" the few years of youth left to her. In other words, she wants to be free to carry on with her younger lover, George, a Republican senator and bachelor from Colorado.

Through the flats I saw them embrace, then scatter as they heard Irene approach. Aware that Jim was in the audience, I entered a door up left, carrying a portfolio under my arm. Always the first entrance was real terror. Blinding lights enveloped me as I was drawn toward the dark gaping hole filled with rows of strange upturned faces. I walked stage center. Somehow words came out of my mouth. A voice, Irene's, not mine, reached out to the last row.

Jim watched as I portrayed this serious young woman with a fine intellect. He hardly knew me, but on stage he saw a competent woman, efficient, studious, uninterested in fashion or romance— exactly my opposite.

As the play moves forward, the plot twists to the edge of fantasy. George explains to Irene that he is in love with a woman whom he cannot marry and cannot name. Irene agrees to marry

George *in name only*—an arrangement which will prevent scandal as he carries on his romance with Constance and furthers his career as a married politician. Irene will receive a large sum of money for her labor and give him a quiet divorce the moment his lover is widowed.

After marriage, of course, unattractive Irene is transformed. As the wife of a senator, she has her hair styled and buys beautiful clothes. Irene becomes inextricably linked to George's career. She can discuss foreign policy and history. She advises him on his speeches, she entertains brilliantly, and because of her charm and intelligence, the White House finds it to their advantage to make George Under-Secretary of State.

George is dazzled and can't help falling in love with this beautiful, intelligent, fascinating woman, whom he still calls Miss Elliot.

I can only speculate on how much Irene's brilliance influenced Jim's opinion of me, but I do know that after playing her for a couple of months, I didn't want to let go of the way it felt to be Irene. I liked being a strong, intelligent woman of integrity, a woman with faith in herself. I wanted to be Irene. Her influence lingered with me for a time, and for a while I felt like Irene.

It never entered my mind, until years later as I wrote about it, that Jim may have fallen in love with Irene.

On opening night I had been twenty years old for six days. After the show, Fiona rushed to greet me backstage. Her usually flushed face was on fire, her thin lips parted in a jagged blood red smile. Panting with excitement, she threw her arms wide, capturing me in her embrace. "You were brilliant!" she breathed. "Perfect!" she gasped, passionately covering my mouth with hers.

I had expected a little hug of congratulations, not a lustful kiss. "Thanks," I gasped, shocked, trembling with shame.

Pressing her considerable bosom and pubic bone against my own, she rubbed noses with me and exhaled, "Wouldn't you like me to help you with costume changes? You have so many, darling." She was caressing my back. I could smell whiskey on her breath. "Between scenes I could wait for you in the dressing room."

On fire with fear and embarrassed, I gently wiggled myself free. "It's just too crowded in that little dressing room as it is, don't you think?"

I fled and for the rest of our run, I made sure I never had to be alone with her.

The opening night review was positive.

Even younger than the hardworking, stick-to-business niece she portrays, Karen Vorbeck showed increasing evidence of stagecraft, rising above the time-honored cliché that to convince the audience a pretty girl is plain, she need only complete her white collar ensemble with horn-rimmed glasses. In a role requiring a dozen subtle transitions of mood, all of them strategic, Miss Vorbeck acted with intelligence and charm.

Roger made the arrangements. It was up to me to get to my appointment with Mitchell Gertz, the agent who had seen me in *Maid to Order*. With Mother hardly able to contain her freeway hysteria, I was a frazzled wreck by the time we arrived at his office.

I remember nothing about Gertz or his office except for the white shuttered doors through which we entered. But I remember the city and how I hated the stinking smog-laced air, the traffic, the ugly street scenes. And I remember the upshot of our meeting.

Gertz said he would consider representing me but that it would be up to me to "knock around Hollywood for a year. Show me how much you want this life. Beat down some doors and get some parts. Then we'll talk about it."

I left his office dazed.

On the drive home, Mother and I discussed the implausibility of his plan.

"I don't want you to do this! Knock around town? You'd have to get a job—good enough to support you. Most actresses have to work as waitresses. In your spare time you'd have to go to auditions. L.A. is huge—you'd need a car—it isn't like New York."

I already knew I didn't have what it took to "beat down some doors." What if the doors had people like Fiona Leeds behind them or worse? I'd heard about the casting couch and was afraid of all those ravenously self-assured theatre people—and the city. I'd never had a real job before, unless I counted my job selling nylons and handbags at Penney's with paychecks so small they weren't checks at all but tiny brown manila envelopes with precious little cash inside.

Gertz's "knock around Hollywood and beat down some doors" terrified me. The memory of my father's voice over the telephone lines at CWC reassured me. "You can always get married."

I didn't need a college education—or a career. I would seek the safety of a marriage. I wasn't afraid of it.

19

Jim

1958 – 1959

"Man! This shower sure feels good! I wish I'd started sooner. Hey, Dad, fix me a drink, will you? Yeah, just a couple ounces of bourbon and some seven-up... Damn! Standing here looking in the mirror you look like some primitive man with short hair. Some guys are born good looking and rich; you're uglier than hell, and poor. Cards are just against you, I guess. Thanks, Dad, thanks a lot. Yeah, it's mixed just right. Usually you make 'em too strong, but this one is just right. Thank yuh, suh. You'd better get on the ball boy. Should leave by at least six-forty. I'd hate to be late on the second date, especially since I was late for the first. Damn you're ugly . . .For cryin-out-loud! It's six-forty-five . . . I've got to take the quickest way out of town." —Jim Ragsdale, *Hot Date*, 1958

JIM WASN'T UGLY, yet when he wrote about getting ready for his second date with me, he probably thought he was. His self-deprecation was not always a joke, and too much real-life hardship had left him feeling truly star-crossed. Even though Jim had barely made it through high school, he wanted a college degree and was forced to attend junior college to bring up his grades. By the time I met him he'd almost finished two successful years: good grades, associate editor of the school's literary magazine, and news editor of the college newspaper. After his substandard scholastic history, those achievements seemed almost miraculous to Jim.

The Ragsdale family lived in one of the many housing developments in sprawling Oxnard, a town built at the edges of gigantic lettuce and strawberry fields. I'd heard the girls in Ojai say that they'd never date a guy from Oxnard. I didn't ask why but guessed that it had something to do with the town's reputation for having more than their share of what we called "juvenile delinquents."

One day after school he drove me to his house. Jim wanted his family to meet me. He parked Ole Bessy on the street and we walked to the front door, past two newly planted and staked ash tree saplings on either side of the front walk.

"Home sweet house," Jim said, unlocking the front door. "Welcome to our humble abode!"

We stepped into a living/dining room furnished with Early American style furniture upholstered brown; two or three small paint-by-number paintings hung out of scale on an expanse of flat white walls. I fought with every fiber of my being not to be judgmental and just kept quiet about the art. If a little lived-in—a stack of unopened mail on the chrome dinette table, a box of Kleenex and pill bottles on an end table, and a magazine rack stuffed with newspapers—the house was clean and orderly. Jim took me on a tour of the kitchen, then showed me his room. Marilyn Monroe's 1954 nude calendar hung over the double bed.

"I used to have to share this bed with my big brother," he explained. "Now it's all mine."

His brother, Little George, was married and away at Fresno State College, where he and his wife lived on her secretary's salary and his football scholarship.

The only other furniture in the room, his student desk, had been purchased at an unfinished furniture shop and stained dark maple. A small gooseneck lamp rested on its uncluttered surface, and one of the chrome dinette chairs was pushed into the kneehole.

"That calendar is a little out of date," I said, pointing to Marilyn.
"It's timeless!" He winked.

When Jim's parents came home, I was suddenly self-conscious. I hoped they would like me. His father, whom everyone called Big George, was a burly Greek with sun-reddened skin and an out-sized belly. He worked as a foreman on one of the lettuce mega-ranches outside Oxnard. His mother, Ruby Mable, was an attractive brunette. Jim had her large brown eyes. She worked at Point Mugu in a civil service office job. Between them there wasn't enough money to help Jim or his brother through college. Both welcomed me warmly and asked me to stay for dinner.

In some ways Jim's mother reminded me of my step-mother. Like Bonnie, Mable fussed over everyone when she served a meal. She had a touch of the South in her voice. I bet myself that she knew how to kill, gut, and fry up a chicken like I'd seen a neighbor lady do back in Grand Junction. Later I would learn that in Arkansas as a child, she'd scrubbed clothes on a washboard more times than she cared to remember and during the Dust Bowl her family packed up and moved to California for jobs as migrant workers.

* * *

One evening at dusk, Jim parked at the beach in Santa Barbara and we walked barefoot down to the water. We laid a blanket on the sand and sat down to watch the sun burn over a red sea. Oil tankers waited like dark scars on the water off shore as sailboats in silhouette headed home.

"You know, Jolene told me something today," he said, to the breeze. She was Jim's old high school chum. "She said I should watch out for you—that you had a reputation as a heart breaker."

"How does she know? She doesn't even know me."

"She said she knew—someone told her something and she wanted to warn me."

"Nice that someone is talking behind my back." I'd never even had a conversation with Jolene. *What has she heard?* I had plenty of guilt about my recent past, especially about what happened with John Turner.

"Well, guess what, I don't care," he said, giving me a hug. "I feel like living dangerously."

We kissed and I felt relieved, grateful, and in love.

We opened another beer and rubbed tar from oil tanker spills off our toes as he told me a high school story.

"Back then, my buddies and I did a fair amount of drinking. On Friday nights one of us would have a trunk full of beer. We'd drag Main looking for friends. Usually we'd pick up girls—and go to the beach to drink. Sometimes we'd take our BB guns and shoot rats down by the pier."

"You did what?"

"A service to mankind." He laughed and went on. "But one night, we picked up a girl we knew was easy. Jack—it was his car—didn't want to be seen with her, so he made her get down on the floor of the back seat till we got out of town. I couldn't believe it," Jim said. "When Jack told her to get on the floor, she just crawled down around our feet, like she knew she was a piece of shit. Jack drove out to the country—to the fields. By the time he stopped the car, Tony had pulled her up off the floor. He was necking with her and had her pants half down—"

"In front of everyone?" I didn't know *this* Jim.

"Yeah, he didn't care. When the car stopped, Ned grabbed her away from Tony, 'Let's all get a piece,' he said. Everyone liked that idea, except me and the girl."

Jim looked at me for a second as if to gauge my reaction. I was thinking about that poor girl and another girl outnumbered and forced to lie on a lawn under a gang of boys.

Lifting the beer to his lips, he stared out to sea. "She started to cry. She looked only a little more scared than me, then ran off across the field. The guys started after her and I ran after them. They had her down on the ground—her pants off and Tony had climbed on while the others held her down. I was yelling for them to stop—yelling that they'd all end up in jail. They weren't listening until I kicked Tony off her and said, 'Look, you're gonna have to fight me first—all of you!'

The girl got up and ran. No one chased her but me. I got ahold of her hand. 'I won't let them touch you,' I said. Come back with me and we'll take you home.' She was whimpering and shaking all over. I climbed into the back seat and put her next to the door so no one else could get near her. I told Jack to get us out of there. The girl didn't want us to take her home, so we just let her off downtown and she ran off into the dark. I never saw her again."

"You were a hero," I said, remembering Frankie and how he'd saved me that night in Lincoln Park. I was afraid to tell Jim that story. Afraid he'd think I was easy, like the girl on the floor of Jack's car.

* * *

From the time he was an eight-year-old newspaper boy, Jim had to work. In high school he'd held a job at the local Frosty Freeze, frying burgers and dipping ice cream. His senior year he'd been vice president of the Boy's Federation and sports editor of the school newspaper, but his high school career had been checkered. He'd done pretty well in classes he liked but kissed off the others. It was doubtful that he would graduate.

"Do you know what my high school counselor told me?" Jim said, his dark eyes hurting. "He said I should be realistic about my potential. He thought I should forget college and get a job as a mechanic or gas station attendant."

By the time Jim had made it through his sophomore year, his father was foreman at one of the big lettuce ranches, responsible for hundreds of thousands of dollars' worth of produce spread over hundreds of acres of land. He watched over every seedling and every weed, spread fertilizers, and sprayed for pests and weeds. It was Big George's decision when to harvest. A bad decision could cost the company big.

One year at harvest time, when Little George and Jim were in high school, he got them jobs. His boys, along with teams of migrant workers, sweated all day in the hot sun cutting heads of lettuce and crating them. At night under lights they hefted the crates onto slow-moving trucks. Jim said they had worked from early morning until the middle of the night, day after day. When the harvest was over, Big George had backed his exhausted sons up against the packing house wall and locked eyes with them.

"If you don't get a college education, this is how you can expect to work for the rest of your goddamn lives."

It had worked. Little George was away at college and Jim was determined to follow him. They were born eleven months apart and he had always admired his big brother, wanted to be just like him. When Little George turned out to be a talented quarterback, Jim wanted to be one too. He made the team, went to all the practices, and worked and played as hard as he could, but at game time he spent most of his time on the bench.

"Finally I got it through my thick head that I wasn't going to be a football star like my brother. So, I said to myself, 'Hell, if I can't play football, then I'll write about it.'" Soon after that Jim began covering sports events for the school newspaper.

The summer before his freshman year in college he'd needed a better job and gone to work at Camarillo State Mental Hospital as an attendant on the men's violent ward where, more than once, he was beaten, strangled, and smeared with feces. I listened breathlessly as he described his dealings with dangerous madmen. He said that as soon as he'd been certain that he was going to get killed, he'd transferred to the children's ward, where he saw a lot more feces and vomit but wasn't faced with mutilation or death. He told me touching stories about the children on the ward, some of whom had been shelved there by parents who didn't want to bother with their problems. He loved the children, and I admired him for wishing he could take his favorite small, lonely boy home.

Jim had triumphed over adversity. He had lived the most interesting life of any boy I had ever known. He could talk about more than sports and cars; he was comfortable talking about his feelings and his life. We shared each other's thoughts and talked for hours about his dreams. I admired what I saw as his calling to journalism, his desire to serve a worthy profession. Most of all I thought I'd found my soul mate.

That summer on one of our drives above Ojai, we went for a walk in the foothills of the craggy Topa Topa Mountains. No matter where we were or what we were doing, Jim had stories to tell. I'd never known a boy who talked so much—he was just as good as a girlfriend. That day as we walked along a narrow road bordered by dusty oaks and dry tufts of grass, he was reminded of childhood and fishing trips to the mountains with his father.

"He took me hunting too. I guess he taught me to shoot when I was six or seven—after I'd started school. Funny, but I started out loving school—before I got fat in seventh grade and everyone called me Fatty."

"You? Fat?"

"Yeah, I was for about two years, then I shot up and got tall like my grandpa. But when I was in the first grade I loved school," he said, laughing at a memory he was about to tell me.

"One day when the teacher asked, 'Who knows the seasons?' I waved my hand in the air, the teacher called on me, and I stood up proud and said, 'Well, there's fishing season, duck season, deer season—' I could've named more, but everyone was laughing at me."

I laughed and took his hand. I could see him as a little boy, bright and earnest, ready to teach the world the things he knew.

Jim was quiet just long enough for us to hear the sound of running water. We stopped to listen and decided there must be a creek just off to our left at the bottom of a gully. We pushed our way through low shrubs and half-slid down a steep bank to a creek bubbling over a rocky bed. We walked along the creek for a short distance and picked up a trail.

"God, it's beautiful here. Let's see where the trail goes," I said, moving ahead of him on the path. Before long we came to a wide, more open place where huge boulders had tumbled into the creek, creating a dam and a large pool of deep water—a perfect swimming hole. We climbed up on a large flat boulder and stretched out in the sun.

We lay there for a while soaking up the warmth from the boulder, silently listening to the sound of water escape from the deep pool and wind its way down the mountain. Jim turned on his side, a bent arm supporting his head, and looked at me.

"Hey, Pretty, I think I'm in love with you," he said, kissing me.

He called me pretty as if it was my name. "I *think* I'm in love with you too."

He laughed and kissed me again. Lately his kisses had made the earth move, and this one shook the boulder beneath us.

"Let's go swimming," he said, taking off his shirt.

"In the nude?"

"Are you shy?"

"No!—Yes," I reconsidered.

"It's hot and the water is cool. It'll be fun. I won't look, I promise."

Jim slid off the stone and took off his shoes and pants. He threw his jockey shorts on the pile and walked to the edge of the water, testing with his foot.

"It feels great. Not too cold." He waded in and swam out to the middle. "I can touch the bottom here. It feels like I'm standing on a big rock. You'll love it. I'll turn around and you come in," he said, coaxing me off the rock.

I took my clothes off behind a shrub. "What if somebody comes? The road is up there somewhere."

"Nobody's going to bother us. We'll splash around and make lots of noise and they'll leave us alone," he shouted over his shoulder.

"Start splashing!" I called as I sank into the cool water.

I swam out toward the middle of the pool, feeling like Eve at the beginning of time. I'd seen enough Esther Williams movies to fantasize what was going to happen next. Jim and I would join hands and in one great burst of energy and grace surface-dive to the bottom of the pool. Just like I'd learned the summer Anne, Sandy, and I did water ballet, we would arch our backs into dolphins, his clockwise, mine counter clockwise and, as our bodies righted, come together in an underwater embrace.

"Can you swim under water?"

"Hell, no."

I let myself sink. The water was clear enough that I could see the rocky bottom of the pond. Jim was standing on a large rock, his bottom shining white where his swimsuit had been. I swam deep enough to see that the pond appeared very deep in places between the boulders. I came up for air and went down for another look. After the boulders had fallen into the creek, the swimming hole had formed in a wide crevice in the creek bed as it traveled downhill. The next time I came up for air I felt Jim pulling me into his arms. He held me from behind, one hand on my belly and another on my breast, pulling me toward the rock. I turned my head to receive his kiss and spun around to face him. We stood on that rock with our heads out of water, holding each other for a long time, kissing, our bare skin touching under water.

I filled up with tears.

"What's wrong?" He lifted my chin for a look at my face.

"I don't know," I said, telling the truth. He kissed me again. And then I knew—it was Reggie—and more. "I've got something to tell you. Let's get out."

"No, tell me now."

I braced myself for the worst. "I'm not—there was someone back in Grand Junction," I said, afraid of what he would say. I could feel tears gathering again. "We went together for about two years—I'm not a virgin." I had to tell him. He would find out. I knew we were going to make love for the first time.

After we'd made love that afternoon at the swimming hole he'd had tears of happiness in his eyes. He said he was glad that what had happened to me had happened a long time ago. It seemed so important to him that Reggie was part of my distant past. I could not tell him about Dan, or—it was too shameful to think of the rest. I had not been completely honest but I had been wise.

"You don't hold it against me?"

"It happened before I met you," he'd said. "Look, I fell in love once too."

I was grateful to Jim for understanding and eager to listen while he told me about a first love as life-altering as mine.

20

The Bad Penny

1952

JIM MET ERIN when he was fourteen and just about to flunk out of El Centro High School. El Centro was a low-lying desert town of about eleven thousand people in the California's Imperial Valley next to the Mexican border. A fruit and vegetable growing paradise, it owed its life to the Colorado River, which brought precious water to them from the mountains of my childhood.

As he told me this story he never mentioned Erin's looks. I don't know if she was pretty, but she came from a better-off family and was a good student—her social standing, her person, everything about her inspired Jim. At about the same time that he wanted to impress Erin, the shop teacher had taken an interest in him, and Jim did well in that class. With both Erin and his teacher rooting for him, he stopped cutting school and brought up some of his other grades. Erin's encouragement and love spurred him on in ways that most of the teachers and his parents could not.

"If it hadn't been for her," he said, "I would have dropped out of school. She believed I was a lot better than I was. I knew that she had enough pride that she wouldn't want to date a drop-out."

In 1954, in the midst of Jim's new enthusiasm for school, his father decided to move the family from El Centro to Oxnard. The development of the vacuum cooling process (which aided in the shipping of produce) brought Big George north to a better job and sent Jim into a tail-spin. He hated leaving Erin, but the next summer, a month before his sixteenth birthday, he hitchhiked nearly three hundred miles back to El Centro to spend the summer near her.

Jim arrived in town hungry and broke, but his pride would not let him knock on Erin's door until he had a job and a place to stay. He walked up and down El Centro's hot, dusty streets looking for work, his belly wrenching with hunger. From the dime store to the grocery store to the coffee shop he stopped to say he was willing to wash dishes, bus tables, sweep up, or stock shelves. He didn't care. Finally a shopkeeper asked if he was willing to finish a painting job and Jim went to work.

I don't know why I can see that room as if I had been there. But when he told me the story I could—the tall windows facing the street, the hot sun puddling brightly on the dirty floor. I could smell the shining white paint Jim used to transform that room into something clean and new. To me, the room symbolized the heart of the young man I believed could transform me too.

At the end of his first day in El Centro, Jim collected his pay and bought dinner. The shopkeeper kept him on for the summer and gave him a place to stay. Jim felt proud of himself—free at last to knock on Erin's door.

"I felt like a real man," he said about his first experience trying to survive on his own. "I reached out to ring her doorbell, knowing I could take care of myself. When Erin's old man answered the door, he looked surprised, then growled, 'The bad penny returns.' He walked off, leaving me standing outside feeling like a pile of shit, wondering how I was going to see Erin. Then I heard him yell, 'Erin, there's someone at the front door.'"

Erin didn't think Jim was a bad penny. She loved him. Ecstatic hours of freedom, being on his own and in love, filled the weeks that followed. But near the end of summer Erin broke up with him. I don't believe he told me the details. He always spoke of her with respect and kept what was confidential between them. But he got on a bus going back north believing that she had lied to him. He'd been crushed, and he blamed everyone for his heartbreak—his parents for being broke, himself for being a low-life, and Erin's father for not giving him a chance. He blamed everyone but Erin.

"She was a victim of how things are," he said. "That's the way the world works and there's no changing it. If you *ain't* the cream, you oughtta to know better than try and rise to the top."

I could see the hurt in his eyes. "I don't believe that's true," I said, hugging him, burying my face in his neck. "You can become whatever you want. You have to believe that. If you don't believe in yourself no one else will."

I'd forgotten where I'd heard that.

*   *   *

One evening outside 601 Shady Lane in Ole Bessy, Jim surprised me with an engagement ring. As a lark some weeks before, we had looked at rings sparkling under lights in a Ventura jewelry store window. I'd made sure that I admired only the smallest diamond rings, so he wouldn't think I was greedy. I don't remember the exact words he used to propose, but they were traditional and in earnest. Something Gregory Peck would have said to his leading lady. Jim was eager to be appropriate, maybe even proper. The quarter carat diamond solitaire set in white gold glittered in the sunlight, the crown jewel of Jim's sweet proposal.

"The jeweler said it's a perfect stone. I knew it couldn't be big, but perfect is even better, don't you think?"

"I love it!" I said, removing it from the box.

"Let me," Jim said, taking it from my hand. He slipped it on my finger and it fit.

I was going to marry my soul mate.

For our engagement announcement, I went to a local photographer to have my portrait made. The announcement appeared in three newspapers: *The Ojai Valley News,* the *Oxnard Press Courier,* and thanks to my grandmother, *The Daily Sentinel.* I hoped that Reggie would see it.

*   *   *

Not long after we were engaged, Jim's mother accidentally called me Erin. Jim looked like he'd been stabbed in the heart and immediately stormed out of the room.

"Oh, my Lord," Mable moaned, "ever since you came along I've tried my best to say Karen instead of Erin and now I've gone and done it."

"It's all right," I said, getting up from the sofa where I'd been sitting beside her. I headed for Jim's room. I found him lying on his bed staring at the ceiling.

"Are you still in love with Erin?" I was scared to hear his answer.

"No!" he insisted. "No."

"Are you sure?" I asked, prepared to give the ring back.

"Yes!" Suddenly sitting up, he took my hand and pulled me onto his lap. "It's just that the sound of her name brings back horrible memories."

Jim would always love Erin; her love had changed his life.

21

One of the Family

IN THE EARLY years, as the Depression wound down, the Ragsdale family struggled to survive even though Big George took any kind of work he could get. He spent one summer picking peaches, but color blindness kept him from seeing which peaches were ripe. At another point, he got a job constructing cement ditches. He was allergic to the lime in the cement and his legs broke out in sores, but the pay was good and he didn't miss a day's work.

Off and on, Mable's health was poor. Once, when she was desperately ill, the hospital turned her away. Big George had no insurance and no money to pay for her treatment. Jim tried to explain his feelings of helplessness to me, the shame that went with being poor.

"You can't possibly understand, because you've never gone hungry. You've never been poor." He stared at the wall, as if looking at me would hurt him.

"But I want to understand."

Years after the fact, the memory of his mother's rejection at the hospital door still filled him with rage. He raised a clenched fist over his head and slammed it on the table.

"Those bastards!"

His eyes misted over as he described his father's life. How he had worked long, hard hours, coming home every night in pain from his bad knees and hips, nearly dead from exhaustion. Jim worried that he would end up like that, and I think I can say with some surety that even after he had graduated college, was Boston Bureau Chief of the Associated Press, and for twenty years editor of the *New Bedford Standard Times*, he still felt the scars of poverty.

For almost as long as he could remember, Jim had worked. His first job as a paperboy had left him with memories of rising before dawn and loading up his bicycle before school. Sometimes he rode through the neighborhoods tossing papers onto front stoops under a pre-dawn sky lit by an atomic bomb exploding in the Nevada desert. Later he shined shoes at a newsstand in El Centro where an old Negro "shoeshine boy" had taught him spit shines.

Proud of this skill, he made me sit down and put my feet up on a stool. He scooped the polish onto his fingers and slapped it to the leather, spitting and rubbing again.

"Sit back and relax. This takes time," he said. "In my time I've been known to use as many as ten layers of polish and spit." Between spits he whistled a tune.

I leaned into my chair and watched the show.

Satisfied at last, he took a brush in each hand and brushed up a shine. Finally bringing out a long, narrow shoeshine rag, he buffed, whistling as he snapped the rag in rhythm like a tap dance. When finished, I could actually see my smiling face in the toes of my shoes.

Later I remembered one day after school in Grand Junction when Reggie handed me a tin of shoe polish and a rag. "Look at my shoes, they need to be polished," he said, sitting down on his bed. Like a servant, I knelt at his feet and went to work. After I had covered every scuff and turned the shoes shiny brown, he teasingly pushed my face to the floor.

"There, slave!" he laughed.

"Yes, master." I joked, trying to push myself up.

"I won't let you up unless you promise to be my slave forever."

"Reggie!" I squealed, "let me up! You're hurting me!"

"Promise to be my slave!" he commanded pushing harder.

"I promise, I promise," I cried. I climbed up off the floor and into his arms sobbing. Didn't he know he had hurt me? "My neck—how could you do that?"

"I didn't mean to, Baby," he said, trying to kiss me. "I love you. You know that, Baby. Look at me. I want to see your smile."

"I don't want to smile!"

I didn't know that when someone loves you he doesn't hurt you.

* * *

"We all have unhappy childhood experiences," Jim's mother said during one of our conversations about her childhood in Arkansas. As a young girl she had cooked noon-day dinner for her farm family and scrubbed the family laundry in a tub and washboard set up outside over the fire. During the Dust Bowl years, her family had joined the great migration from Oklahoma and Arkansas to California. They were called "Arkies." Seven of them crowded together in an old combination truck and school bus her Poppa had welded together. Groaning with the weight of mattresses, the old washtub, Grandma's treadle sewing machine, and all things necessary to their survival, they headed for deep southern California.

"On our way, a fast-speeding road hog caused Poppa to veer and turn over. I wasn't hurt bad, but my brother's wife was pregnant and had to be hospitalized a few days. Our California relatives sent a semi-truck to pick us up." Mable wrote about those years and shared her writing with us.

"None of us escapes unhappiness," Mable said.

Sometimes when we were alone, she'd tell me her unhappy stories. I loved listening to Mable's gentle Arkansas twang, as she revealed her life, her fears, her hopes, her feelings. Mable talked to me like my mother could not.

Big George cooked a barbecue once a week, and I was invited. He fired up his kettle-shaped Weber grill, and once it had settled to glowing coals, he roasted a moist smoky turkey or a large roast beef on the spit, the fat coated with his own blend of herbs. He cooked thick steaks or chicken on the grill. There were always baked potatoes and Mable's iceberg lettuce salads rich with ripe avocado off their tree and the dark red tomatoes George brought home from a farm stand. Her creamy egg and potato salad sweetened with tiny bits of sweet pickle and spiced with mustard was my favorite. We would sit down together at the chrome dinette set and enjoy the delicious food and wine. I felt like part of the family, especially when they started up with their stories.

"One night," Jim said, "when Dad was walking home from the store—in those days he couldn't afford a car—he found a billfold lying beside a curb with a roll of dollar bills—$25.00—a whole week's wages. Remember that, Dad?"

"Sure do," Big George grunted, heaving a big sigh, "brought it home to Mom." Unless he was in the mood to talk, Jim's father always spoke as if he barely had the strength for the effort. But when he was in the mood he'd hold court, weaving one long complex sentence into another until no one else could get in a word.

"We looked through the billfold for some kind of identification," Mable clarified. She didn't want me to think they were thieves. "But there wasn't any—so we kept the money. It was the spring of the year," Mable went on. "Easter was coming and I wanted to buy Jim and Little George Easter suits. I took them down to King's Department Store and got them fitted into white linen suits. Remember those suits, Jim?"

"How could I forget," he groaned. "You kept letting them out. Then you cut off the pants and made them into shorts. I thought we'd never outgrow them."

"I was expecting your sister at the time, so I bought myself a pretty blue maternity dress." The thought of that blue dress made her eyes dance. "That Easter we got all dressed up and went to our first Easter sunrise service."

"It's a good thing you have that story to tell, Mom," Jim said, "because there aren't too many happy memories."

Big George's work in El Centro wasn't always steady. Sometimes he had to go as far away as Wisconsin to find work. He'd be gone for months at a time. Sometimes Mable held a job, like the time she cashiered at the drugstore.

"Once, when Big George was away, I ran out of money and food. I didn't know what I was going to feed you kids. Remember that, Jim?"

"Sure," he laughed. "You picked all the worms out of an old box of oatmeal. Then you cooked it and fed it to your poor unsuspecting children."

"You were hungry," she chuckled. "The only other thing I could find in the cupboard was a jar of tomatoes and we had some margarine in the fridge. So I warmed up the tomatoes and served the oatmeal on the side with margarine on top. You ate every bite!"

"Remember how in El Centro we used to have to look for scorpions in our beds every night before we went to sleep?" Jim said.

"Do I! Now and then I still catch myself looking between the sheets before I get into bed!" She laughed at the memory. "Do you remember when..." and she was ready to tell another amazing story—something awful that happened long ago that they could finally laugh about.

* * *

Sometimes Mable and I would sit on the couch together with our teacups, sipping her percolated coffee as she told me stories about the days when her children were young, about all the places they had moved as George searched for work. Even though they didn't have a car, at one time they lived at the El Centro Auto Court, where Big George could walk to work and carry groceries home from town.

"There was a large canal directly in back of our place. I was afraid my boys would drown, so much of their playtime had to be indoors," Mable remembered. "That wasn't much fun for two small boys so I invented an unusual way for Jim and Little George to play outside with their buckets and shovels. I put them under the shade trees at the side of our place. I couldn't keep an eye on them at that location unless I was outside, so I tied each one of them to a tree. The caretaker of the place had dug small ditches to water the shrubbery and trees. Lots of times I would let Jim and Little George sit by the ditch and dangle their feet for a while. I'd keep an eye open for the manager," she laughed. "I didn't want to get caught. But one day he came to the door wild with anger and ordered me to keep my 'damn kids' out of the water. I didn't like what he called my boys, so I grabbed a broom and hit him on his head."

Mable and I really liked each other, even though her curiosity made me uncomfortable at times. She'd ask all kinds of questions. "Why do you want to get married—give up your chance to be an actress?" she asked with an almost dazed expression. "Tell me what it's like to stand in front of an audience." She looked dizzy at the thought. "Your mother, Bette—she's so—so different." She hoped she hadn't used the wrong word. "I like her," she jumped to say, "She's always so friendly. We had lunch the other day—did she tell you? She wouldn't tell me about her book. She seemed shy about it. How long's she been writing it anyway? What's it about?" And Mable had an inclination to stare at me. Every now and then I'd catch her and she'd smile or try her best to avert her eyes, or sometimes she'd just giggle and confess, "I'm sorry, Karen, I can't help staring at you—you're so pretty."

I could tell she had been a pretty girl herself. Old pictures confirm it. And at that time, in her forties, she was a pretty woman with a trim figure, dark curly hair and warm, almost black, eyes. But Mable was a nervous woman, haunted by a life full of disappointment. She worked hard to elevate her spirits, to find the good in every setback, to never burden others with her cares. I've never known anyone who tried so hard to be cheerful. She was kind to a fault, and I loved her.

22

Backstage

"Perhaps it is better to wake up after all, even to suffer; than to remain a dupe to illusions all one's Life." —Kate Chopin

THE FALL OF 1958 I enrolled at Ventura College again and went to work as a part-time switchboard operator at the *Ventura Star Free Press*. From the very first day I hated the job. The switchboard was located near the front door, behind the receptionist's desk, where everyone could see me blunder around trying to make the lights stop blinking. I had an awful time remembering where to plug in the calls, to discern which of those myriad little round holes in long straight rows would connect to phones on the copy desk, the editor's office, or the advertising department. I'd asked for a diagram with names to help me learn, but they never got around to providing it. When the switchboard lit up like a Christmas tree I'd panic and plug in anywhere handy just to get rid of the callers. The job reminded me daily that I was a failure. I *looked* efficient and quick, but phones rang on the wrong desks all over that building.

I had no interest in my classes—I wanted to be on stage. But the Art Center hadn't had a part for me since my supporting role in *The Tender Trap*. After three months, I dropped out of classes and in

January I gave two weeks' notice at the paper. I can't believe they didn't fire me first.

I took a job working full time for Dr. Bee, Ojai's veterinarian. Except for cage cleaning duties, I was happy there. I did everything from receptionist work to assisting the doctor in surgery. During surgery, I looked away as I lifted a shaking hand to offer his surgical tools. Once I assisted, brokenhearted, as he put a whole litter of pups to sleep. But I was good at welcoming patients and their owners, holding and soothing dogs and cats while he gave them shots, and comforting them when it was over.

The Art Center announced its next play, *Born Yesterday*. Both Jim and I showed up for auditions. I wanted to play Billie Dawn. Jim knew how much time I spent at the Art Center when I was in a play. He decided to try his hand at acting so we could go to rehearsals together. They cast him in a small part, the barber.

The director didn't even want to hear me read for Billie. He looked at me like I was a child and winked. "Honey, you ain't lived enough to play that gal."

I wanted to throw out one hip, give it a wiggle, and ooze, "Wanna bet, buster!" But I was afraid to be a smart aleck.

"I can use a good prop master," he said, "help us out backstage!"

I didn't want to be prop master but I didn't want to look like a bad sport, so I took the position. Fueled by the energy of my burning frustration, I micro-managed props backstage. While Jim rehearsed his lines behind the footlights, I collected, organized, and distributed towels, razors, whiskey bottles, and books as if those objects would save the world. Through the flats I watched a good-looking redhead in her mid-thirties rehearse her lines. She used a nasal Brooklyn accent and vacant expression—except for the hair, a Judy Holliday rip-off.

I'd be a perfect Billie. I know how to be a dumb blonde. I'd been trained to play Billie on Catalina, where I'd learned the accent—if only I hadn't dieted myself down to nothing and still had Marilyn's hair. If only the folks at the theatre hadn't typed me as the ingénue.

*   *   *

She'd kept quiet as long as she could, but Mother was not happy about my engagement to Jim. "He'll end up just like his father!"

"What do you mean?"

She was pacing. "Poor!" she shouted.

I was stunned by her snobbery. "How do you know that?"

"I know! You are a star and he's not! Anyone can see that," she said, stopping long enough to glare at me.

"He will not be poor! He's going to college and when he gets out he'll be the editor of a newspaper—we'll live in a nice town somewhere and raise children." It sounded like a good life to me.

"Look at you now! He's on stage and you're backstage. Do you want to be backstage the rest of your life? What about *your* career? *Your* education?"

"I don't want to 'knock around Hollywood.' We agreed that I can't do that!" I burst into tears. "I'll get a job and put Jim through school, and we'll—"

"What are you making now?" she interrupted. "Nothing! Not enough to live on. You've never had a good paying job. You are such a dreamer!"

We fought about Jim almost every day.

It was right around that time that Mother burned all four hundred pages of her novel. She didn't have much of an answer when I asked why, saying something about being a fool for thinking she could write that book. To burn it was so final, and so like her. She destroyed the evidence leaving nothing behind to show that she had tried and failed. The level of her anguish, the obliteration of all those hours and all that hope, horrified me. But, at that point, I had little real sympathy for her.

* * *

Jim and I had decided that just like Little George and his wife Mary Lou, Jim would go to college and I would get a job to support us. It did not occur to me that he might have gotten the idea from his brother. It may have appeared that way to my mother, but if it did, she didn't say so. I had come along at the perfect time to help Jim go on with school. I did not question the timing of that or of Jim's arrival on the scene just when I had given up on myself, when the realities of a professional stage career had scared me away, when I was looking for a way out and marriage had been offered.

I didn't think about Erin and how Jim had depended upon her to pull him through or ask myself if this was a pattern—that he might have needed me like he'd needed her. In those days there were no Pell grants or scholarship funds except for exceptional students, or the GI Bill for men who had done a tour of duty in the military.

"I'm going to support you for two years, and you're going to support me for the rest of my life! Sounds like a good deal to me," I'd say with a laugh.

We had agreed that after he had graduated and was working, I would go back to school to study. I didn't know what. Besides, Jim wanted to do something important. He felt about journalism like I had felt about the theatre before I was scared away. He was going to do something of value to the world. Together we would solve both our problems. I truly wanted to help him. He would be my calling.

23

You Are a Married Woman Now

"Every human being on this earth is born with a tragedy, and it isn't original sin. He's born with the tragedy that he has to grow up...." —Helen Hayes

THE NIGHT I found the note on my pillow, I tried to imagine myself on a plane to New York City. I tried to see myself on my own, hurrying down a squalid street to an audition exhausted from working all night as a waitress. I saw myself standing in a long line of pretty girls, hoping that I'd get a break. Then I thought of the men I'd have to out-manipulate, run from, or give in to. I didn't want a career on the stage that badly. I was terrified of the whole thing and wanted to be safely married to Jim.

> Dear Karen,
> I have $350.00. You can have it to get on a plane and go as far away from Jim as you can. Go someplace new and make a new start for yourself—or you can have it for your wedding. It's your choice.
> I love you,
> Mother

Knowing how my father felt about paying for college, I was afraid to ask him for money for a wedding. I wanted the money mother offered and I wanted her blessings. Because she offered only half of what I wanted, I ripped the note to pieces. That night, as I rolled in and out of sleep, I knew what I would tell her in the morning.

* * *

There were too many problems: Mother's attitude about the marriage and Daddy's attitude about money. Spending $350 on a wedding seemed wasteful to Jim and me—especially with my mother standing by joyless. I didn't want to say my vows in the presence of her doubt. We decided we would elope and spend some of the money on our honeymoon. The rest would go toward settling us in San Jose, where Jim had been accepted at San Jose State. An out-of-town friend suggested that we get married at his church in Glendale, eighty miles south of Ojai.

For my wedding dress I decided on the luxury of a dressmaker. I bought a pattern for a street-length sheath dress with a matching jacket and several yards of ivory satin brocade. I was not a virgin so I didn't even think of wearing white. Pearl earrings, a little hat with silk flowers, and gloves and shoes to match completed my ensemble. I still have the dress and almost every day bump into the earrings in my jewelry box.

Once I had given her the news, my mother said nothing about my wedding plans. She moved around the house like a shadow, spending most of the time in her room, her tongue bloody from biting it. The tension in the air had come to feel like the house on Third Fruitridge in Grand Junction. By my wedding day the air was thick with hostility (mostly mine). I packed my large bag and cosmetic case and dressed in the going-away dress I had made for the occasion. Eager to get out of the house, I waited in the driveway for Jim to pick me up. Together we had made a down payment on a brand new Renault.

My mother came to the front door with her camera. She took a picture of me standing beside her car with a cigarette in my hand and the suitcase at my feet. I looked thin, scared, and very young.

We changed into our wedding clothes at the Methodist church in Glendale. I popped a white carnation in Jim's lapel, and he pinned a white orchid on my shoulder. While we waited in a little chapel we read telegrams from Grand Junction and one from Shady Lane.

"Dearest Karen and Jim. Love to you both. Mother, Susan and Gretchen."

I wanted to cry.

At last our matron of honor and best man came through the chapel door, Little George and his wife Mary Lou. I didn't know either of them very well but wanted to love them. I looked up to Mary Lou, a successful supporting wife of a college student.

We were married in a haze of words and gestures that could not break through my numbness. I wondered if Jim was numb too. No emotions came to signal the beginning of my new life, no sentiment for the life that I was leaving. All I could think was *Mother and my sisters aren't here.*

Jim had made dinner reservations at a fine dining restaurant nearby. From a plush tufted booth straight out of a forties film noir, we listened to strolling violins as our best man and matron of honor toasted us with champagne.

We spent our wedding night in a motel room just big enough for a double bed. We even took a picture of it draped, as it was, with a deep pink chenille bedspread. When we climbed into bed I felt like I was doing something wrong. I wanted Jim to hold me while I cried, but didn't know how to tell him that I was feeling my mother's sadness. I could see her face buried in her hands, disappointed in me again. After we made love, as lonely moonlight fell through the unfamiliar window, I lay there worrying, feeling guilty. Had I made a terrible mistake? *A wedding night isn't supposed to be like this.* I was sure.

By the time the sun rose, I had hardly slept at all. Jim stirred and finally woke up. I pretended to be cheerful, to look like a happy bride should look, and we made love again. I felt much better and wondered why I'd been in such a state all night.

"Hey, Pretty, I can't believe that you belong to me now."

"We belong to each other," I said, kissing him.

Over a hearty breakfast and our road maps I got interested in the journey we were about to make. Our destination was Grand

Junction, only three days away, but we were going to take three weeks for our honeymoon. Jim had never been east of Bakersfield.

We drove across Nevada, stopping to take pictures of the Joshua trees and a little tourist trap with a donkey we could pet. We toured Hoover Dam before heading north to Zion National Park in Utah, where we arrived after dark.

By the car's headlights we somehow made camp. We didn't have a tent, but we lit a fire, opened a can of baked beans, roasted wieners, and after our supper settled into our double sleeping bag under the stars. It was a cold late-March night, and I told Jim a story.

"There was this guy—he was camping alone in the desert—not that far from here. It was a cold night—kind of like tonight—so he zipped himself up in his sleeping bag. In the morning when he woke up he found a rattlesnake had crawled inside and cuddled up beside him to keep warm."

"You can't scare a fella who used to kick scorpions out of bed." Jim laughed and rolled on top. "I can't believe," he whispered in the dark, "that all I have to do is put out my hand to touch you."

The sun jolted us awake early. As our eyes took in soaring walls of red rock lit by early morning sunlight, we cuddled together, warm in our sleeping bag, awed by the wonders around us. We had camped close to a canyon wall. Under the soft morning sky, massive red sandstone towers rose above us. In deep red shadows gnarled pinyons bent above dusky sagebrush and tufts of yellow grass appeared through patches of snow. As far as Jim was concerned, we were on another planet. I had grown up around these landscapes, but he had never seen earth and stone the color of brick or skies that color of blue.

After we cooked our breakfast over a campfire, we took a hike with our camera, wandering below sandstone fortress walls, towers, and minarets eroded over millions of years by wind and water.

That night in Salt Lake City we saw the Mormon Temple lit to look like the heavenly city. Our next stop would be Grand Junction and the La Court Hotel—I'd always wanted to stay there. But when we drove down First Street to Main we found that the lovely old hotel, the monument to high society as it existed in the Grand Junction of my childhood, had been torn down. An ugly fifties modern La Court Motel stood in its place. We stayed one night.

Out on Third Fruitridge, when I introduced Jim to my father for
the first time, Daddy reared back on his heels, rocked up on his toes,
and growled, "I understand you've been sleeping with my
daughter!" Jim paled. I laughed. My father grinned and patted Jim
on the back. "Welcome to the family, son!"

After I showed Jim around Third Fruitridge, the canal, Peggy Ann's
house, the high school, and downtown Grand Junction, my father
loaned us his Jeep for a trip into the mountains. Gleefully, I showed Jim
the sights of my childhood summers in Redstone. We stopped to walk
in the snow along the Crystal River and peeked into windows at the
Helgersons' cottage. Holding hands, we walked the dirt road to the
general store and I made him eat a Fudgsicle. On the way out of town
we drove as far as we could through snow to take pictures of the
Redstone mansion surrounded by a field of white snow.

* * *

My grandmother pinned a white orchid to my dress. She stroked my
cheek and kissed me. She embraced Jim and, flirting, said, "My
word, but you're a handsome fellow."

The family was eager to get to know my husband and celebrate
the wedding. My grandmother had made dinner and bought a small
wedding cake decorated with fresh daffodils. My aunt and uncle
were there with my cousins, and Daddy and Bonnie and eighteen-
month-old Kristen joined them in the living room. Everyone had
dressed up for the occasion. Jim and I wore our wedding clothes. I
could tell that they liked and admired my new husband.

After dinner, we had wedding cake and opened gifts in the
living room. That's when the subject of our return trip to California
came up. We had decided that because of the threat of bad weather
we should take a southern route.

"Look," my father said, "you really ought to go by way of Telluride.
It's a fascinating place. When I was on the road doing sales for
Vorbeck's I used to stop at the Sheridan Hotel. It's a beautiful old place
built in the Gay Nineties. The town is full of history—in the good old
days every other business on Main Street was a whorehouse."

The drive up to Telluride, over high mountain passes and through the snow, was long and treacherous. We hadn't seen another car on the road for what seemed like fifty miles. Jim had never driven in a snowstorm, and the going was slow. As dusk approached the snow came faster and Jim turned on the windshield wipers. Snowflakes raced at the windshield like millions of little white darts thrown at us through the headlights. We crept down the mountain hoping we were on the right road. Finally, coming to level ground and a dark, deserted town.

We drove up and down the main street looking for the Sheridan Hotel. A large three-story square brick building loomed above us. Jim got out of the car and, straining to see through the falling snow, found the painted words "New Sheridan" barely visible on the face of the brick. The place looked deserted.

We opened the hotel door and peeked into the dark lobby, cheered by the sight of one bare light bulb hanging over the front desk. We walked over creaking floorboards toward the light and tapped the bell on the desk. An old woman dressed in a bathrobe and slippers appeared from a back room.

"We'd like a room for the night," Jim said, sounding doubtful.

The old woman had Jim sign in, then grabbed an ancient key off the rack and motioned for us to follow her up the main staircase to the second floor. With each step we could feel the slanting staircase tremble. She showed us into a gigantic room with five old iron beds — three singles and two doubles, all with visibly lumpy mattresses. Before she could leave us, I asked if there was a restaurant in town where we could have dinner.

"Nope," she shrugged, "but if you go on down to the pool hall he'll make you some sandwiches." We thanked her and she disappeared.

Jim trekked through the snow to the empty pool hall, got our ham and Swiss on white bread sandwiches and some beer, and brought them back to our room. By then my father's joke was apparent, but we weren't laughing. Dazed, we sat on the edge of one of the beds to eat.

"I'm afraid this is my father's sense of humor."

"Well, we made it over the mountain and we aren't cold or hungry—or dead," Jim reasoned, "so let's make the best of it. Have another beer and then we'll have another. This is a honeymoon, so we'd better take advantage of all these beds."

"All five?"

"You bet!" he said trying to reach for me.

I was already leaping from bed to bed in my stocking feet, jumping up and down on squeaky mattresses, calling, "Come and get me!"

* * *

On our way back to California we saw the ancient city built of adobe and stone snuggled into a stone cleft on the cliffs at Mesa Verde. We stopped at the south rim of the Grand Canyon and, continuing our pilgrimage into our childhoods, drove on to El Centro, the dusty desert town where Jim had been a boy. That night we went out on the town, drank tequila, and danced to a mariachi band in a raunchy old Mexicali bar. I'd never seen anything so exotic.

The next day we visited with his relatives at their house on the outskirts of town. His uncle, a rough, scary-looking man with leathery skin stretched over a skull-like face, was sunburned brown everywhere but his forehead from working outdoors in a hat. When I answered his aunt's questions about myself and my family, his uncle looked at me like I was from Mars. I'm sure he thought I talked funny. But Jim was pleased when his uncle took him aside.

"You done good to marry that gal, Jimmy boy," he said. "You can take her anywhere."

Before the day was over all the cousins came to meet me and to congratulate Jim with slaps on the back. We spent the evening out on the porch listening to them play guitar and sing songs like *Cotton Fields* and *Big Rock Candy Mountain*.

Jim's round-faced aunt rocked in her rocker as she sang. "There's a dark and a troubled side of life; there's a bright and a sunny side, too…" Her strong voice left me mesmerized by those words sung in her Arkansas accent. She knew all about the troubled side of life.

Everyone picked up the beat and sang, "Keep on the sunny side, always on the sunny side, keep on the sunny side of life…"

"Oh, the storm in its fury broke today, crushing hopes that we cherished so dear, storms and clouds will in time pass away, the sun again will shine bright and clear." Cousin Ronnie played and sang so well that everyone said he could be a star at the Grand Ole Opry.

Jim took a turn. "Let us greet with a song of hope each day though the moments be cloudy or fair..." He looked happy. His eyes were alight with love for his family and the memories that came with that old song.

Even though I felt like I was in a foreign country, to this day that evening on the porch is a joyful memory for me.

*   *   *

Golden California poppies and red geraniums bloomed in the flowerbed at 223 South San Clemente. The sun dazzled off the white stucco walls as we moved into our first home—a one-bedroom duplex across from the DeSoto Plymouth Dealership in Ventura. Back from our honeymoon, it was time to look for jobs. We wouldn't go off to college until fall.

Jim took a job with Mastercraft Laundry driving their delivery truck and a part-time job with the *Oxnard Press Courier* as a stringer. I got a job at Sears in sales. We bought a few pieces of furniture for very little money: a pale blue damask club chair, a white Naugahyde sofa— sleek and modern—a floor lamp, a bed, a chrome dinette set, and a gas stove from the 1930s. We had purchased art prints from the museum in L.A. and thumbtacked a Toulouse-Lautrec and a Marc Chagall to our bare white walls. We didn't have enough money for more than two prints so we hung an empty frame on one wall.

I dialed my mother as soon as I got home. Her voice came warm and cheerful across the line. Not long after we spoke she was standing on our doorstep smiling, her arms open to receive me.

"Come in, Mother," I said, pressing her close. "I've missed you."

"I've missed you too, honey. You look wonderful," she said, holding me at arm's length for a look. Jim had come into the room from the kitchen and stood there beaming at us.

"Son Jim," she said, hugging him. "I've always wanted a son."

That was it. For better or for worse she'd made her protest and it was over. For the rest of her life Jim had no better friend. Years later she told me, "I was no good at picking husbands for my girls."

On our first-month wedding anniversary, I picked marigolds and red geraniums and arranged a bouquet for our table. I made my own spaghetti sauce from scratch and set the table with place mats and candles. Jim grinned, delighted with himself for remembering to surprise me with a small bottle of champagne. I looked over his shoulder, cowering as he bounced the cork off the kitchen wall. He poured the champagne into water glasses and raising his glass said, "Here's to the best month of my whole life!"

"I'll drink to that!" I said. We hugged and sat down to dinner at our chrome dinette set under the empty frame on the wall.

We had decided that together we were going to read every good novel we could find until we were both well-read. Every night we climbed into bed and before going to sleep read aloud to each other. Our first book was *A Tree Grows in Brooklyn*.

I became interested in cooking and loved poring over recipes and dazzling Jim with my culinary skills. Mable taught me how to make her crispy fried chicken and creamy egg and potato salad. She showed me how to iron Jim's dress shirt, saying how pleased she was not to have to do them anymore. I liked cleaning my little house and washing my pretty new dishes and putting them neatly away in the cupboard. On our days off I did laundry and Jim took out the trash and helped me clean up the house. And every night we climbed into bed with a book and read each other to sleep.

* * *

One afternoon I was in the kitchen studying a recipe in my *Betty Crocker Cookbook* when the phone rang. It was Roger Clark.

"We're putting together a production of *Maid to Order* in L.A. We've got Maureen O'Sullivan for Susan, and Michael O'Shea will play Charles. We haven't cast Danny yet, but we'd like you to reprise your role as Nancy." He said something about me not being a member of Equity and that there wouldn't be much pay, but after I heard him say that he'd like me to play Nancy, I didn't hear anything else. My head swam around those delicious words, *we'd like you to reprise your role. . .*

"Well, Roger, you know I'm married now."

"I heard," he said cheerfully. "How's married life?"

"Good. We just got settled after our honeymoon."

"Well, I suppose you'll want to talk this over with your husband."

"Yes, I will. It sounds wonderful—I just don't know how we'd manage. Let me talk to Jim. I'll call you back."

Jim was at work. After Roger's phone call I was alone for a couple of hours, my mind swirling over possibilities and impossibilities as I finished up household chores and worked on dinner.

I wanted to play Nancy again—this time in the city with important actors. Maureen O'Sullivan was famous for her role as Jane in the old Tarzan movies. Michael O'Shea was a well-known character actor married to Virginia Mayo.

It would be an experience of a lifetime, one handed to me without my having to beat down anyone's door. *But how would I get to rehearsals every day? How would I earn the money we needed for Jim to go to college?* I had forgotten to ask the date of the opening and my salary. *Maybe the show would have a long run and Jim would have to go off to college alone for a while.*

Minutes before I expected Jim, I opened a can of button mushrooms and drained them. They would go in the sauce for the chicken I was roasting. By the time he walked through the door I was so excited that I spilled the whole story before he could sit down.

His reaction was immediate and unwavering. "We are married now. You can't go running off to L.A. to be in a play."

"But maybe I could," I said, frantically, like playing Nancy was a matter of life and death to me. "Maybe we could work it out. Let me just get more details from Roger before we decide."

"You can't go to L.A. alone. I'm going to San Jose in a month. How would you live down there—we can't keep two places—we've already made our plans. You are a married woman now—you already made your choice."

His words spun around me like a tornado. I dropped down on the sofa and sat there still, saying nothing, staring at my hands, unable to feel my feet on the floor. I raised my eyes to his face. He was frowning at me. Suddenly everything was clear.

"You're right," I suddenly understood. "Of course, you're right," I said as got up to go to the kitchen. "It's all right, Jim." I had to check on dinner.

Alone, gripped by the hurt, I saw the irony of it all. The moment I had stopped striving, I was gifted with another chance. I had grown up enough to realize it was just another wild goose chase. Nothing more promising than a chance to feel the adrenaline rush again. I didn't want to feel hurt and disappointed anymore. I wanted to be a good wife to Jim; I couldn't think of myself first anymore. I had made promises and had responsibilities, a home to keep, a husband.

I reminded myself that I should be proud. Roger thought I was good and he called me. I had been his first choice. I would call him after dinner and tell him no.

Consulting my cookbook, I melted butter in a saucepan and sautéed the mushrooms. I made a roux, whisked in chicken broth, and watched it thicken. Then I added cream. I had been a good actress—maybe even exceptional—but I had made my choice. I would leave for San Jose in the fall and would not look back. I can say now, almost sixty years later, that I never regretted not having a life in the theatre.

My *velouté* sauce with mushrooms was ready. It looked perfect. The chicken roasted with potatoes and carrots was perfect. All I had to do was make the salad.

I went to the kitchen door and called, "Honey, would you like a drink before dinner?"

* * *

Jim and I moved to San Jose in late August. On an earlier trip, we had found a new apartment building in need of a manager. We got the job and, in payment, an apartment for only $25.00 a month. Jim enrolled in classes, and it was time for me to find a job. I opened up the newspaper and looked at the want ads, scanning the columns for the best wage I could find. The highest paying job by far was at the

American Can Company—a file clerk for $369.00 a month. I called and made an appointment.

Sales office manager Jack Anderson's office (in one of those old-fashioned glassed-in rooms off a large sales office) was on the second floor of a big tin can factory in a dubious part of town. He asked about my experience. I told him about selling hose at Penney's and Sears and helping out at Dr. Bee's. We talked a little about Jim and his plans. He told me that he had interviewed an exhausting number of girls for the position, but he was going to hire *me*, and didn't I want to know why?

"Yes, why?" I was stunned.

"See those girls out there in the office?" He pointed through the glass to the sales room where four men and two women sat at wooden desks. One of the women looked to be in her late thirties and the other in her mid-twenties, both very attractive.

"You're the first girl I've interviewed that I know will get along with them," he said. Looking as relieved as I felt, he leaned back in his chair. "We can teach you the job in no time, but it's important that you fit in here. Ruth and Barbara are very classy girls."

I had a job! I got the first job I applied for—the one with the biggest paycheck! I could hardly wait to tell Jim. My job as a file clerk at the American Can Company would give us enough money. For the first time since grade school Jim would not have to work. He could study and be a real student. I felt very much like a useful, grown-up member of society.

I did fit into the sales office; Ruth, Barbara, and I became best friends. And every now and then I had to smile when I thought of the second reason Mr. Anderson had given for wanting to hire me.

"Besides," he'd said, smiling like a fox, "You look great in that straight skirt."

ACKNOWLEDGMENTS

The beginning of this book goes back twenty-some years when I came face-to-face with the fact that I'd had an unusual childhood worth writing about. My first editor/teacher was Penelope Franklin who helped me understand something about memoir writing. Unfortunately, I've just learned that Penne died before this book could be published. Saddened, I must thank her for all her help. I have to mention two friends who read the first draft and still speak to me. Thank you, Janet Freedman and John Chamberlain. Heaps of gratitude go to Jennifer Currier who insisted that attempting to fictionalize my memoir was a mistake. She, Andie Armstrong, Ben Keefe, Helene Messina, and Cory MacLean read my first drafts and encouraged me forward. Deep appreciation goes to Laurel Busch, my editor, and Jodi Thompson and Twyla Beth Lambert at Fawkes Press. I thank my father, Herman 'Miles' Parsons Vorbeck, for being a good provider, for patiently talking me down from the top of the tallest cottonwood tree in Colorado, for dancing lessons, and for my life. Most of all, I want to thank my mother, Bette Burgess Vorbeck, for her determination to live life as an artist and for being the wonderfully eccentric woman she was.

Did you find an error in this book?

Fawkes Press strives to present a perfect product, but being staffed by mere humans, mistakes happen. If you find something we missed, please visit www.FawkesPress.com and click on "bounty program," to submit your find and enter to win our quarterly bounty.

FAWKES PRESS

CPSIA information can be obtained
at www.ICGtesting.com
Printed in the USA
FSHW021252170720
72241FS